THE PAIN AND THE ITCH

by **Bruce Norris**

Cast in order of appearance
Mr Hadid **Abdi Gouhad**
Clay **Matthew Macfadyen**
Kelly **Sara Stewart**
Kayla **Hannah Gunn/Shannon Kelly/Angelica Trew**
Cash **Peter Sullivan**
Kalina **Andrea Riseborough**
Carol **Amanda Boxer**

Director **Dominic Cooke**
Designer **Robert Innes Hopkins**
Lighting Designer **Hugh Vanstone**
Sound Designer **Paul Arditti**
Assistant Director **Amy Hodge**
Casting Director **Amy Ball**
Production Manager **Paul Handley**
Stage Manager **Andy Ralph**
Deputy Stage Manager **Maddy Grant**
Assistant Stage Manager **Nafeesah Butt**
Stage Management Work Placement **Laura Williams**
Dialect Coach **Jan Hayden Rowles**
Costume Supervisor **Jackie Orton**
Set Built and Painted by **Souvenir Scenic Studios**

The Royal Court and Stage Management wish to thank the following for their help with this production: Angel Flowers Islington, Early Learning Centre, www.egamma.co.uk, Habitat, Heals, www.holdall.co.uk, Alan Jenkins, Nigel Makin, Marks & Spencers, Partridge's, Peter Jones, Waitrose.

The first major UK revival of two
ground-breaking plays first performed
at the Royal Court in the 1960s.

Performed in Repertoire

21 September – 15 December

rhinoceros

by Eugène Ionesco

In a new translation by **Martin Crimp**
Direction **Dominic Cooke**
Design **Anthony Ward**

Sponsored by **Coutts & Co**

1 November – 15 December

the arsonists

by Max Frisch

In a new translation by **Alistair Beaton**
Direction **Ramin Gray**
Design **Anthony Ward**

020 7565 5000
www.royalcourttheatre.com
Royal Court Theatre, Sloane Square, London SW1

ARTS COUNCIL
ENGLAND

THE COMPANY

Bruce Norris (writer)
The Pain and the Itch was first performed at Steppenwolf Theatre, Chicago, in 2004. Other plays include: The Infidel, Purple Heart, We All Went Down to Amsterdam, The Unmentionables (Steppenwolf Theatre, Chicago); adaptation of Up Against It, The Vanishing Twin (Lookingglass Theatre, Chicago).

Bruce has also worked with Philadelphia Theatre Company, Playwrights Horizons (New York), The Galway Festival (Galway, Ireland) and this autumn he will be working with Woolly Mammoth Theatre, Washington D.C.

Awards include: Whiting Foundation Prize for Drama 2006; two Joseph Jefferson Awards (Chicago) for Best New Work; 2006 Kesselring Prize, Honorable Mention.

Paul Arditti (sound designer)
Paul has designed the sound for over 70 productions at the Royal Court since 1993. Recent designs include: Nakamitsu (Gate); Vernon God Little, The Respectable Wedding, generations (Young Vic); The Year of Magical Thinking (Broadway); There Came A Gypsy Riding, Enemies (Almeida), Tempest (Tron); Market Boy (National); The Bee (Soho); Herge's Adventures of Tintin (Young Vic at The Barbican); Billy Elliot (Victoria Palace); The Crucible (RSC); Festen (Almeida/West End/Broadway); trade (RSC/Soho); As You Like It (RSC/Novello); Mary Stuart (Donmar/West End); A Girl in a Car with a Man (Royal Court); Blood Wedding (Almeida); Sleeping Beauty (Young Vic/Barbican/Broadway); Six Pictures of Lee Miller, Just So (Chichester); The Pillowman (National/Broadway).

Awards include: Olivier Best Sound Design Award 2006 for Billy Elliot; Evening Standard Best Design Award 2005 for Festen; Drama Desk Outstanding Sound Design Award 2005 for The Pillowman.

Amanda Boxer
Theatre includes: An Arab Israeli Cookbook (Gate/Tricyle); Macbeth (Arcola); The Destiny of Me (Finborough); The Graduate,

The House of Bernarda Alba (Gate/Gielgud); The Touch of the Poet (Young Vic/Comedy); A State of Affairs (Duchess); The Merchant of Venice, The Importance of Being Earnest, All My Sons (Young Vic); The Yiddish Queen Lear (Southwark Playhouse/Bridewell); The Holocaust Trilogy (New End); No Shame and No Fear (Jermyn Street); Come Blow Your Horn, The Fall Out Guy, Absurd Person, Singular, The Misanthrope, Present Laughter (Manchester Royal Exchange); An Ideal Husband (Theatr Clwyd); Death and the Maiden (Library, Manchester); One Last Card Trick (Watford).

Television includes: Bodies III, Trial and Retribution III & VII, The Shell Seekers, Kipling: A Remembrance Tale, The Fall Out Guy, Chalk, Cider with Rosie, The London Embassy, Put on by Cunning, Miss Marple, Sleeping Murder, Sense and Sensibility.

Film includes: Saving Private Ryan, United 93.

Dominic Cooke (director)
For the Royal Court: Other People, Fireface, Spinning into Butter, Redundant, Fucking Games, Plasticine, The People are Friendly, This is a Chair, Identical Twins.

Other theatre includes: Pericles, The Winter's Tale, The Crucible, Postcards from America, As You Like It, Macbeth, Cymbeline, The Malcontent (RSC); By the Bog of Cats (Wyndham's); The Eccentricities of a Nightingale (Gate, Dublin); Arabian Nights (Young Vic/UK and world tours/New Victory Theatre, New York); The Weavers, Hunting Scenes From Lower Bavaria (Gate); The Bullet (Donmar); Afore Night Come, Entertaining Mr Sloane (Theatr Clwyd); The Importance of Being Earnest (Atlantic Theatre Festival, Canada); Caravan (National Theatre of Norway); My Mother Said I Never Should (Oxford Stage Co./Young Vic); Kiss of the Spider Woman (Bolton Octagon); Of Mice and Men (Nottingham Playhouse); Autogeddon (Assembly Rooms).

Opera includes: The Magic Flute (WNO); I Capuleti E I Montecchi, La Bohème (Grange Park Opera).

Awards include: Laurence Olivier Best Director and Best Revival Awards 2006 for

The Crucible; TMA Award 2000 for Arabian Nights; Fringe First Award 1991 for Autogeddon; Manchester Evening News Award 1990 for The Marriage of Figaro. Dominic was Associate Director of the Royal Court 1999–2002 and Associate Director of the RSC 2002–2006. Dominic is the Artistic Director of the Royal Court.

Abdi Gouhad

For the Royal Court: Pirates, The Lion and the Jewel.

Other theatre includes: Gadaffi (ENO); Baby Doll (National/Albery); The Cinnamon Veil, Tales of a City, Hippolytus, The Love of the Nightingale (Theatre Melange); South Sea Bubble (Connaught, Worthing); Toys in the Attic (Watford Palace); Mrs Bailey Goes to War, Scenes from Soweto, The Titanic (Theatre Foundry); Black Lear (Temba, UK tour); How We Held the Square, Jack and the Beanstalk (Arts); Miss, Open Air Picture Show, Abracadabra, Doing It, Tales from Whitechapel (Common Stock, UK tour); A Midsummer Night's Dream, A Taste of Honey (Salisbury); The Tempest (Mermaid).

Television includes: Waking the Dead, Casualty, Lost Empires, Dr Who.

Film includes: Dirty Pretty Things, I'll Sleep When I'm Dead, Welcome Home, You Can Run …, Rollerball.

Radio includes: Nineteen Eighty Five, Passion Child, Ukay, Travelling Down the Nile.

Amy Hodge (assistant director)

For the Royal Court: My Child.

Other theatre includes, as director: The Ethics of Progress (Unlimited Theatre/ Oxford Playhouse); The Tempest (Orange Tree Theatre schools tour); Kick for Touch (Orange Tree Theatre); Theatre of Change (Congrieve Room, West Yorkshire Playhouse); Influenced (Etcetera); Vagina Monologues (Leeds City Variety Music Hall).

Theatre includes, as assistant director: Tangle (Unlimited Theatre Co.); The Hoxton Story (The Red Room).

Amy was trainee director at the Orange Tree Theatre 2005-2006.

Robert Innes Hopkins (designer)

For the Royal Court: Redundant, Other People.

Theatre includes: Senora Carra's Rifles, Miss Julie (Young Vic); Our Country's Good (Liverpool Playhouse); Carousel (Chichester Festival Theatre); Promises, Promises (Crucible, Sheffield); The Water Engine (Young Vic/Theatre 503); Singin' in the Rain (Sadler's Wells/Leicester Haymarket); Macbeth (RSC); Julius Caesar, Pinocchio (Royal Lyceum, Edinburgh); The Resistible Rise of Arturo Ui (National Actors' Theatre, New York); Romeo and Juliet, The Villain's Opera (National); The Tempest, Present Laughter, The Seagull, The Wasp Factory (West Yorkshire Playhouse); Othello (Washington Shakespeare Theatre); My Mother Said I Never Should (Oxford Stage Co./tour); The Weavers, Hunting Scenes from Lower Bavaria (Gate); Happy End (Nottingham Playhouse); A Servant to Two Masters, The Comedy of Errors, The Malcontent (RSC/West End).

Opera includes: Rigoletto (Lyric Opera of Chicago); Betrothal in a Monastery (Glyndebourne); Die Soldaten (Ruhr Triennale); Peter Grimes, Simon Boccanegra, Wozzeck, The Italian Girl In Algiers (Santa Fe Opera); Cavalieri Rusticana, Il Pagliacci (Deutsche Oper, Berlin); The Flying Dutchman (WNO/Opernhaus Zürich); Manon Lescaut (Opera North/Opera Oviedo); Passion (Minnesota Opera); The Cunning Little Vixen (Bregenz Festival, San Francisco Opera); La Boheme, I Capuleti e i Montecchi (Grange Park Opera); Charodeika (Teatro Nacional de Sao Carlos); The Elixir Of Love (Opera North/WNO); Rigoletto (WNO); Paradise Moscow (Opera North); Mr Emmet Takes a Walk (Orkney Festival); The Bartered Bride (Opera North/ Opéra National du Rhin); Les Miserables (Tel Aviv Arts Centre).

Film includes: Lucia di Lammermoor.

Awards include: TMA Best Design Award 2006 for Promises, Promises; 1996 Critics' Circle Designer of the Year Award for The Comedy of Errors and Weavers; 1997 TMA Designer of the Year Award for The Wasp Factory and My Mother Said I Never Should.

Matthew Macfadyen

Theatre includes: Henry IV Parts 1 and 2 (National); Battle Royal (National); School for Scandal, A Midsummer Night's Dream (RSC); The Duchess of Malfi, Much Ado About Nothing (Cheek by Jowl).
Television includes: Secret Life, The Project, Spooks, The Way We Live Now, Perfect Strangers, Warriors, Wuthering Heights.
Film includes: Incendiary, Death at a Funeral, Middleton, Pride and Prejudice, In My Father's Den, The Reckoning, Enigma, Maybe Baby.

Andrea Riseborough

Theatre includes: Miss Julie, Measure for Measure (Theatre Royal, Bath/RSC); Citizenship/Burn/Chatroom (National); A Brief History of Helen of Troy (Soho).
Television includes: Party Animals, Mrs Beeton, Doc Martin, A Very Social Secretary, Whatever Love Means.
Film includes: Untitled Mike Leigh 2007, Magicians, Venus.

Sara Stewart

For the Royal Court: Etta Jenks.
Other theatre includes: Proof (Donmar); A Month in the Country, Troilus and Cressida (RSC); There are Crimes and Crimes (Leicester); Out Cry (Cheek by Jowl); The Real World (Soho Poly); Temptation (Westminster); Cat on a Hot Tin Roof (Lyric, Belfast); Arms and the Man, The Crucible, Entertaining Mr Sloane (Summerstock, USA).
Television includes: Robin Hood II, Sugar Rush I & II, Midsomer Murders, Life Begins, A Very Social Secretary, A Touch of Frost, Waking the Dead, Taggart, Wire in the Blood, Holby City, Monarch of the Glen, Auf Wiedersehen Pet, Los Dos Bros, NCS Manhunt, Meaningful Sex, Chambers, Inspector Rebus, Too Much Sun, People Like Us, Supply and Demand, Hetty Wainthrop Investigates, Space Island One, Crocodile Shoes, Men Behaving Badly, Anna Lee, Dr Finlay, The Good Guys, Taggart, Minder, Poirot, The House of Elliott.
Film includes: Medium Rare, Act of God, The Road to Guantanamo, A Cock and Bull Story, Batman Begins, London Voodoo, Mrs Brown, The Winslow Boy, Three Blind Mice.

Awards include: Emmy Award 2006 for Sugar Rush I & II; Rhody Best Newcomer Award for Arms and the Man.

Peter Sullivan

For the Royal Court: Rock 'n' Roll (& Duke of York's), Stoning Mary.
Other theatre includes: Mercy (Soho); Lulu, Certain Young Men (Almeida); Drummers (Out of Joint/New Ambassador's); La Bete Humaine (Nottingham Playhouse); The Bacchae (Opera Factory); Way of the World (Lyric, Hammersmith); King Lear, Richard III, Napoli Millionaria (National); Runners, Musicians, Alien Activity (National Studio); Action Replay, Measure for Measure, Our Town (Contact, Manchester).
Television includes: The IT Crowd, Wire in the Blood III and IV, A Very Social Secretary, Extras, The Brief, The Last Detective, Nathan Barley, Sex Traffic, Single, State of Play, Close and True, Strange, Always Be Closing, Hope and Glory, Heat of the Sun, Kavanagh QC, Peak Practice, Rules of Engagement, Lord of Misrule, Sometime Never, Backup I and II, Chandler and Co., Devil's Advocate, Date Rape, Over the Rainbow.
Film includes: Chromophobia, Puritan, Monsieur N, Out of the Game, Conspiracy, Christie Malory's Own Double Entry, The Day of the Jackal, Young Indiana, El Effecto Mariposa.

Hugh Vanstone (lighting designer)

Theatre includes: Boeing Boeing, Epitaph for George Dillon, Then There Were None, Mary Stuart, Bombay Dreams (West End); Rafta Rafta ..., Market Boy, The Royal Hunt of the Sun, Once in a Lifetime, The Pillow Man, Howard Katz, Life x3, The Cherry Orchard, The Day I Stood Still, Closer, The Homecoming (National); Spamalot (Las Vegas/Broadway/US tour/London); Tanz der Vampire (Berlin); The Philadelphia Story (Old Vic); Grand Hotel (Donmar); The Deep Blue Sea (Exeter).
Awards include: Olivier Best Lighting Designer Award 2004 for Pacific Overtures (Donmar); Olivier Best Lighting Designer Award 2000 for The Graduate (West End) and The Cherry Orchard (National); Oliver Best Lighting Designer Award 1998 for The Unexpected Man (RSC) and The Blue Room (Donmar).

AWARDS FOR
THE ROYAL COURT

Martin McDonagh's The Beauty Queen of Leenane (co-production with Druid Theatre Company) won four 1998 Tony Awards including Garry Hynes for Best Director. Eugene Ionesco's The Chairs (co-production with Theatre de Complicite) was nominated for six Tony awards. David Hare won the 1998 Time Out Live Award for Outstanding Achievement and six awards in New York including the Drama League, Drama Desk and New York Critics Circle Award for Via Dolorosa. Sarah Kane won the 1998 Arts Foundation Fellowship in Playwriting. Rebecca Prichard won the 1998 Critics' Circle Award for Most Promising Playwright for Yard Gal (co-production with Clean Break).

Conor McPherson won the 1999 Olivier Award for Best New Play for The Weir. The Royal Court won the 1999 ITI Award for Excellence in International Theatre. Sarah Kane's Cleansed was judged Best Foreign Language Play in 1999 by Theater Heute in Germany. Gary Mitchell won the 1999 Pearson Best Play Award for Trust. Rebecca Gilman was joint winner of the 1999 George Devine Award and won the 1999 Evening Standard Award for Most Promising Playwright for The Glory of Living.

In 1999, the Royal Court won the European theatre prize New Theatrical Realities, presented at Taormina Arte in Sicily, for its efforts in recent years in discovering and producing the work of young British dramatists.

Roy Williams and Gary Mitchell were joint winners of the George Devine Award 2000 for Most Promising Playwright for Lift Off and The Force of Change respectively. At the Barclays Theatre Awards 2000 presented by the TMA, Richard Wilson won the Best Director Award for David Gieselmann's Mr Kolpert and Jeremy Herbert won the Best Designer Award for Sarah Kane's 4.48 Psychosis. Gary Mitchell won the Evening Standard's Charles Wintour Award 2000 for Most Promising Playwright for The Force of Change. Stephen Jeffreys' I Just Stopped by to See the Man won an AT&T: On Stage Award 2000.

David Eldridge's Under the Blue Sky won the Time Out Live Award 2001 for Best New Play in the West End. Leo Butler won the George Devine Award 2001 for Most Promising Playwright for Redundant. Roy Williams won the Evening Standard's Charles Wintour Award 2001 for Most Promising Playwright for Clubland. Grae Cleugh won the 2001 Olivier Award for Most Promising Playwright for Fucking Games.

Richard Bean was joint winner of the George Devine Award 2002 for Most Promising Playwright for Under the Whaleback. Caryl Churchill won the 2002 Evening Standard Award for Best New Play for A Number. Vassily Sigarev won the 2002 Evening

Standard Charles Wintour Award for Most Promising Playwright for Plasticine. Ian MacNeil won the 2002 Evening Standard Award for Best Design for A Number and Plasticine. Peter Gill won the 2002 Critics' Circle Award for Best New Play for The York Realist (English Touring Theatre). Ché Walker won the 2003 George Devine Award for Most Promising Playwright for Flesh Wound. Lucy Prebble won the 2003 Critics' Circle Award and the 2004 George Devine Award for Most Promising Playwright, and the TMA Theatre Award 2004 for Best New Play for The Sugar Syndrome. Richard Bean won the 2005 Critics' Circle Award for Best New Play for Harvest. Laura Wade won the 2005 Critics' Circle Award for Most Promising Playwright and the 2005 Pearson Best Play Award for Breathing Corpses. The 2006 Whatsonstage Theatregoers' Choice Award for Best New Play was won by My Name is Rachel Corrie. The 2005 Evening Standard Special Award was given to the Royal Court 'for making and changing theatrical history this last half century'.

Tom Stoppard's Rock 'n' Roll won the 2006 Evening Standard Award for Best Play and the 2006 Critics' Circle Award for Best Play. Lucy Caldwell won the 2006 George Devine Award and a Special Award in the 2007 Susan Smith Blackburn Awards for Leaves. Alexandra Wood won the 2007 George Devine Award for The Eleventh Capital.

ROYAL COURT BOOKSHOP

The Royal Court bookshop offers a range of contemporary plays and publications on the theory and practice of modern drama. The staff specialise in assisting with the selection of audition monologues and scenes. Royal Court playtexts from past and present productions cost £2.
The Bookshop is situated to the right of the stairs leading to the ROYAL COURT CAFE BAR.

Monday to Friday 3 – 10pm
Saturday 2.30 – 10pm
(Closed shortly every evening from 7.45 to 8.15pm)

**For information telephone 020 7565 5024
or email: bookshop@royalcourttheatre.com**

Books can also be ordered from our website www.royalcourttheatre.com

THE ENGLISH STAGE COMPANY AT THE ROYAL COURT

The English Stage Company at the Royal Court opened in 1956 as a subsidised theatre producing new British plays, international plays and some classical revivals.

The first artistic director George Devine aimed to create a writers' theatre, 'a place where the dramatist is acknowledged as the fundamental creative force in the theatre and where the play is more important than the actors, the director, the designer'. The urgent need was to find a contemporary style in which the play, the acting, direction and design are all combined. He believed that 'the battle will be a long one to continue to create the right conditions for writers to work in'.

Devine aimed to discover 'hard-hitting, uncompromising writers whose plays are stimulating, provocative and exciting'. The Royal Court production of John Osborne's Look Back in Anger in May 1956 is now seen as the decisive starting point of modern British drama and the policy created a new generation of British playwrights. The first wave included John Osborne, Arnold Wesker, John Arden, Ann Jellicoe, N F Simpson and Edward Bond. Early seasons included new international plays by Bertolt Brecht, Eugène Ionesco, Samuel Beckett and Jean-Paul Sartre.

The theatre started with the 400-seat proscenium arch Theatre Downstairs, and in 1969 opened a second theatre, the 60-seat studio Theatre Upstairs. Some productions transfer to the West End, such as Tom Stoppard's Rock 'n' Roll, My Name is Rachel Corrie, Terry Johnson's Hitchcock Blonde, Caryl Churchill's Far Away and Conor McPherson's The Weir. Recent touring productions include Sarah Kane's 4.48 Psychosis (US tour) and Ché Walker's Flesh Wound (Galway Arts Festival). The Royal Court also co-produces plays which transfer to the West End or tour internationally, such as Conor McPherson's Shining City (with Gate Theatre, Dublin), Sebastian Barry's The Steward of Christendom and Mark Ravenhill's Shopping and Fucking (with Out of Joint), Martin McDonagh's The Beauty Queen Of Leenane (with Druid), Ayub Khan Din's East is East (with Tamasha).

Since 1994 the Royal Court's artistic policy has again been vigorously directed to finding and producing a new generation of playwrights. The writers include Joe Penhall, Rebecca Prichard, Michael Wynne, Nick Grosso, Judy Upton, Meredith Oakes, Sarah Kane, Anthony Neilson, Judith Johnson, James Stock, Jez Butterworth, Marina Carr, Phyllis Nagy, Simon Block, Martin McDonagh, Mark Ravenhill, Ayub Khan Din, Iamantha Hammerschlag,

photo: Stephen Cummiiskey

Jess Walters, Ché Walker, Conor McPherson, Simon Stephens, Richard Bean, Roy Williams, Gary Mitchell, Mick Mahoney, Rebecca Gilman, Christopher Shinn, Kia Corthron, David Gieselmann, Marius von Mayenburg, David Eldridge, Leo Butler, Zinnie Harris, Grae Cleugh, Roland Schimmelpfennig, Chloe Moss, DeObia Oparel, Enda Walsh, Vassily Sigarev, the Presnyakov Brothers, Marcos Barbosa, Lucy Prebble, John Donnelly, Clare Pollard, Robin French, Elyzabeth Gregory Wilder, Rob Evans, Laura Wade, Debbie Tucker Green, Levi David Addai, Simon Farquhar, Bola Agbaje, Alexandra Wood, Lucy Caldwell, Polly Stenham, Mike Bartlett and DC Moore. This expanded programme of new plays has been made possible through the support of A.S.K. Theater Projects and the Skirball Foundation, The Jerwood Charity, the American Friends of the Royal Court Theatre and (in 1994/5 and 1999) the National Theatre Studio.

The refurbished theatre in Sloane Square opened in February 2000, with a policy still inspired by the first artistic director George Devine. The Royal Court is an international theatre for new plays and new playwrights, and the work shapes contemporary drama in Britain and overseas.

The Royal Court's long and successful history of innovation has been built by generations of gifted and imaginative individuals. For information on the many exciting ways you can help support the theatre, please contact the Development Department on 020 7565 5079.

PROGRAMME SUPPORTERS

The Royal Court (English Stage Company Ltd) receives its principal funding from Arts Council England, London. It is also supported financially by a wide range of private companies, charitable and public bodies, and earns the remainder of its income from the box office and its own trading activities.

The Genesis Foundation supports the Royal Court's work with International Playwrights.

The Jerwood Charity supports new plays by new playwrights through the Jerwood New Playwrights series.

The Artistic Director's Chair is supported by a lead grant from The Peter Jay Sharp Foundation, contributing to the activities of the Artistic Director's office. Over the past ten years the BBC has supported the Gerald Chapman Fund for directors.

American Friends of the Royal Court are primarily focused on raising funds to enable the theatre to produce new work by emerging American writers. AFRCT has also supported the participation of young artists in the Royal Court's acclaimed International Residency. Contact: 001-212-946-5724.

ARTS COUNCIL ENGLAND

26 JULY - 8 SEPTEMBER 2007

An evening of high drung and slarrit

ABSURDIA

DONMAR

Director
DOUGLAS HODGE

Designer
VICKI MORTIMER

Lighting Designer
PAULE CONSTABLE

Sound Designer
CAROLYN DOWNING

A triple-bill of
British Absurdist
comedies

A Resounding Tinkle
By N.F. Simpson

Gladly Otherwise
By N.F. Simpson

The Crimson Hotel
A new play by Michael Frayn

THE PAIN AND THE ITCH

Bruce Norris

The Pain and the Itch was originally commissioned by the Philadelphia Theatre Company (Sara Garonzik, Producing Director).

The Pain and the Itch received its world premiere at the Steppenwolf Theatre Company, Chicago, IL (Martha Lavey, Artistic Director; David Hawkanson, Executive Director). It was directed by Anna D. Shapiro; the scenic design was by Dan Ostling; the costume design was by Janice Pytel; the lighting design was by James F. Ingalls; and the sound design was by Rob Milburn & Michael Bodeen. The cast was as follows:

MR HADID	James Vincent Meredith
KELLY	Mariann Mayberry
CLAY	Zak Orth
KAYLA	Lillan Almaguer
	and Darragh Quinn Dolan
CASH	Tracy Letts
KALINA	Kate Arrington
CAROL	Jane Houdyshell

The Pain and the Itch received its New York premiere at Playwrights Horizons (Tim Sanford, Artistic Director). It was directed by Anna D. Shapiro; the scenic design was by Dan Ostling; the costume design was by Jennifer von Mayrhauser; the lighting design was by Donald Holder; the sound design was by Rob Milburn and Michael Bodeen. The cast was as follows:

MR HADID	Peter Jay Fernandez
CLAY	Christopher Evan Welch
KELLY	Mia Barron
KAYLA	Ada-Marie L. Guitierrez
	and Vivien Kells
KALINA	Aya Cash
CASH	Reg Rogers
CAROL	Jane Houdyshell

4

Characters

CLAY

KELLY

KAYLA

CASH

KALINA

CAROL

MR HADID

ACT ONE

Afternoon. Snow falls outside. KELLY *and* CLAY *sit side by side on the sofa.* CLAY *holds the* BABY. *They both stare at* MR HADID, *who holds his face in his hands and sobs quietly. This goes on for some time. Finally:*

MR HADID. I am sorry.

CLAY (*rapidly*). No.

KELLY (*the same*). Don't.

CLAY. It's okay.

KELLY. It is *so* okay.

CLAY. More than okay. You should feel absolutely –

KELLY. However you need to . . . however the feelings have to . . . I mean, it's *loss*, for God's sake.

CLAY. And that *loss*, the *grief* that arises from *loss* . . . it would be unnatural to try to *suppress* –

KELLY. You can't.

CLAY. You can't do that.

KELLY. It's *harmful* to do that.

CLAY. It is. No. What you're doing. It's the right thing, and an emotion, I mean, this is something we've been working on. The importance of honouring emotions in the moment that . . . (*To* KELLY.) What?

KELLY *is trying to stop him.*

What? I'm *agreeing* with you.

She mouths some words to CLAY.

(*Quietly, to* MR HADID.) I thought we were in agreement.

MR HADID *wipes his eyes.*

MR HADID. I am better now.

CLAY. But what we wanted to say was –

Then the BABY *starts crying. Loudly.*

Uh-oh. Hey now. Hey, mister.

KELLY. I'll do it.

CLAY. Hey, Mister Angry Face.

KELLY. Clay.

CLAY. I got him.

KELLY. Let me do it.

CLAY. Whatsamatter, Groucho? Hey, Groucho Marx.

KELLY. Clay.

CLAY (*laughing*). Ohh, he's *mad*, isn't he? Look at that face! Grrrrr!

KELLY. Would you let me do it?

CLAY. Heyyy. Shhh.

KELLY. Please just give him to me.

CLAY (*handing* BABY *over to* KELLY). He's stopping. He's stopping.

KELLY. Well, don't *bounce* him.

MR HADID. Now I make *him* cry.

KELLY. No, no, no. Not you.

CLAY. I was only shushing *him*.

KELLY. We didn't mean *you*.

CLAY. No, he just gets a little hyper if he doesn't sleep through the night, but you should go ahead and . . . (*To the* BABY.) Huh? Feeling better now, huh? Yeah. (*To* KELLY.) I wasn't *bouncing*.

KELLY. Jiggling, anyway.

During this, KAYLA has come downstairs, unnoticed. She picks up the TV remote and presses a button. The TV screen is filled with cartoons of clowns and loud children's music fills the room. The BABY cries more loudly.

CLAY (*loud, to* KAYLA). Sweetie?

KELLY. Honey?

CLAY. Kayla?

KELLY. Not now, sweetie.

CLAY. Later, okay?

KELLY. We can watch that later, is that okay?

CLAY. After the grown-ups are done.

KAYLA switches off the set, extracts the tape and calmly leaves the room.

KELLY (*to* KAYLA, *as she leaves*). Thank you, sweetie.

CLAY (*the same*). That's very nice of you. Very polite.

KELLY (*the same*). You're very thoughtful.

CLAY. Very considerate.

She is gone. The BABY has stopped.

MR HADID. You were going to say?

KELLY. Yes.

CLAY. Yes. So. Okay. So the situation was: the day before. We're having breakfast.

KELLY. I had just started going back to the office again.

CLAY. It's the Tuesday before the holiday, and he (*Re. the* BABY.) had just been born and she's on her way into the office in the morning and I'm making breakfast, I'm making eggs for Kayla.

KELLY. And Kayla goes, Mommy *look*.

CLAY. *Shrieks*, and says it.

KELLY. And I look, and there in her hand, right out of the *bowl* on the table –

CLAY. Kitchen table.

KELLY. This bowl has *avocados* in it and one of these avocados has been, what? Has been –

CLAY. – let's just say *gnawed*.

KELLY. *Gnawed* on.

CLAY. Extensively gnawed *upon*.

KELLY. Right down to the *pit*, has been *consumed*. Something, some sort of –

CLAY. Non-human.

KELLY. Unless you know some *human* that bites into an avocado like it was an *apple*, all right? So, yes, some *non-human creature* has entered our *house* and is now *feasting* on our avocados.

CLAY. And of course the mind devises these *scenarios*.

KELLY. But the bottom line is: *one*, what sort of *toothed creature* are we dealing with; *two*, what is the point of *entry*; and *three*, where exactly is it *now*?

MR HADID. Do you have a pet?

Pause.

KELLY (*an uncomfortable subject*). Uhhh . . . no.

CLAY. No.

KELLY. No.

CLAY. No, we . . .

KELLY. No, although Kayla loves hamsters, about which I have said absolutely not.

CLAY. What with the allergies.

KELLY. No. Clay used to have a cat. But there's toxoplasmosis.

CLAY. From the litter box.

KELLY. First trimester, harms the foetus.

CLAY. *Potentially.*

KELLY. *Can* harm.

CLAY. It's not a certainty, but –

KELLY. It's a risk.

CLAY. A *low* risk.

KELLY. Not a risk I *personally* would want to take.

CLAY. Not that I'm questioning the decision because ultimately it is a *life* we're talking about and you have to ask yourself, do I give priority to a *cat's* life? Or to . . . to . . . to . . . ?

KELLY. To a human life.

CLAY. Right. Right. Right. So. Right. So, we made the decision. *I* made the decision.

KELLY. You can say we.

CLAY. To have him killed.

KELLY (*to* MR HADID). Some people might say put to sleep.

CLAY (*laughs*). Well, I mean, he's not exactly *sleeping*, is he? He's *dead*, right? Chester is *dead* now and and and –

KELLY. Clay.

CLAY. And *we did it*. Or rather, the *vet*, at our request.

KELLY (*to* MR HADID). He was euthanised.

CLAY. So, no. We don't have pets.

KELLY. But if you see this on your kitchen table. Your *child* sees it. *Touches* it. And admittedly, I am someone who tends to, on occasion –

CLAY. Overreact.

> KELLY *silently stares straight ahead.*

> Well, honey, I mean . . . (*Laughs.*) I mean, at least *fixate.*

KELLY (*to* MR HADID). We're being so rude. Can I get you something?

MR HADID. I am fine.

KELLY. We have seltzer. Or iced tea.

CLAY (*to* KELLY). Or those green tea things in the bottles.

KELLY. Or caffeine-free Diet Coke. Or with.

CLAY (*to* KELLY). Or bottled water. Or tap water.

MR HADID. I am fine.

> *Uncomfortable pause.*

CLAY. It just means a lot to us that you would –

MR HADID (*interrupting*). Unless you have some apple juice?

KELLY. Oh! Uhhh . . . ?

CLAY. Do we?

KELLY. No. Just. Well.

CLAY. Not the good kind.

KELLY. We have, what is it, like *Mott's*?

MR HADID. It is apple juice?

KELLY. Yeah.

MR HADID. I will have that, thank you.

> KELLY *and* CLAY *both stand.* KELLY *exits, taking the* BABY. CLAY *sits.*

CLAY (*for lack of anything better to say*). *I* used to have a beard. Years ago. Seriously. My dad had a moustache. But on *me*, with the shape of my face, I always thought the full beard. Kelly, though, she . . . didn't so much care for it. But I could grow another. One of these days.

Pause.

It's just, we want you to get an accurate picture of who we are. Which is so hard because you're tempted to fall back on clichés. Which is frustrating if you want someone to understand the things that motivate you. Or all of us. As a people. (*He laughs.*) Well. There you go. Sounds clichéd. No, what I mean is . . . That this society, our society, as a whole . . . (*Flailing.*) Okay. Once again. What does that *mean*? Society as a whole? I don't even know what that *means*. I can only talk about *us*. The things that motivate *us*, because –

MR HADID (*raises his hand*). Excuse me? I cannot stay terribly long.

CLAY. But . . . the others are going to be here.

MR HADID. I have a little time.

CLAY. Especially Mom.

MR HADID. I have some time.

CLAY. And . . . didn't you want the *juice*?

MR HADID. Perhaps you could finish the story of the avocados.

CLAY. Exactly. Yes. So: that was Tuesday. Wednesday, I call the exterminator. And then, of course, it was Thursday, which was the holiday.

Lights change. Snow stops. Evening. It is now Thanksgiving. Tasteful home-entertainment music begins to play. KAYLA, now wearing a party dress, runs through the room, shrieking. She is being chased by KALINA. CASH enters from the kitchen.

CASH. Why do you rule out a *squirrel*?

CLAY. No. They came. They looked everywhere. They said it's not.

CASH. The squirrel is a foraging animal.

CLAY. They said this is something that has an appetite for *fruit*. Which to them did not suggest a squirrel.

CASH. *Fruit?*

CLAY. Yes.

CASH. Avocado's a vegetable.

CLAY. The fruit of the avocado tree.

CASH. Tree?

CLAY. Yes.

CASH. Think it's a *bush*.

CLAY. And even if it *was* a squirrel –

CASH. Could've been nuts in the vicinity.

CLAY. Even if it was.

CASH. Squirrel comes around, he's *foraging* for nuts, gets *distracted* by the avocado –

CLAY (*overlapping*). It's *not*, but . . .

CASH (*continuous*) – gets to that avocado pit, squirrel's thinking, hey, I just discovered the motherfucking Hope Diamond of nuts.

CAROL *enters from the kitchen carrying a pretty tablecloth.*

CAROL. Clay, who is the actor, the one, you know, the one who does the narration for the nature shows?

CLAY. Uhhh . . . I don't know.

CAROL. The one with the baritone voice?

CLAY. I don't know.

CAROL. Because there was a nature show on the other night and it was all *about* squirrels.

CLAY. It's not a squirrel, all right? It's not.

CASH. Rodent of some kind.

CLAY. But even *if*. Still. That's a vector of disease. There's the droppings. There's fleas.

CASH. Avocado's a vegetable.

CLAY. There's lice. And I'd rather not have that around my children, okay?

CAROL (*exiting to the kitchen*). Anyway, that man, the one I meant, with the baritone voice? Well, he *narrated* that show.

Again, KAYLA *runs through the room with* KALINA *chasing her.* KAYLA *is screaming with laughter.*

KALINA (*to* KAYLA). I am going to get you! You not fast enough! Ha! I will capture and torture you!

They almost crash into KELLY, *who enters carrying place settings as they tear through the room.*

CLAY (*calling after them*). Not too loud, sweetie. Your brother's still sleeping, okay?

KELLY (*to* CLAY, *not* CASH, *whom she ignores*). I just wish you had called the other place. That's all I said.

CLAY. You asked me to call and I called. You didn't say –

KELLY. Of *course* they're cheaper if they use *neurotoxins*.

CLAY. You didn't specify. You just said call. You said handle it –

KELLY (*overlapping*). Might as well spray Agent Orange on our children.

CLAY (*continuous*). – which I *did*, so don't act like I'm incompetent.

KELLY (*searching in a closet*). Your mother needs that big salad bowl. And I did say specifically no glue traps.

CLAY. I took them out. I took them out.

KELLY (*from inside*). I just don't think that allowing your daughter watch an animal writhe to a slow sadistic death in a puddle of glue is the best way to solve the problem.

CLAY. You know, if I happen to handle things my own way –

KELLY, *while digging through the closet, has pulled out a set of golf clubs.*

KELLY. Clay, you hired her. Can you explain to that woman the notion of a kitchen?

CLAY. Maybe she doesn't understand what you're saying.

KELLY. Well, then tomorrow we can hire a *translator* for the cleaning person. (*Calling.*) Carol? I found it.

KELLY *exits.*

CASH. Hey, Clay.

CLAY (*calling after her*). But see, do I come to your office and criticise the way *you* do things?

CASH. Got yourself some golf clubs, I see.

CLAY (*still calling*). If I'm the person here every second except three hours a week? Is that unreasonable?

KELLY *re-enters holding the chewed-on avocado.*

KELLY (*lowered voice*). You do *see* this, right? You see *teeth marks*, all right? This isn't *academic*. It's about your *children*. So, at the *moment*? Whether or not you're reasonable? That actually isn't the *topic* right now.

MR HADID *interrupts from across the room. Music stops. Lights change.*

MR HADID. May I ask a question?

CLAY. Oh. Sorry.

KELLY. Of course.

CLAY. Absolutely.

KELLY. Yes, please . . . Anything that's not clear.

MR HADID. I have seen these shoes.

CLAY. These what?

MR HADID. The shoes you are wearing.

CLAY. I . . . you mean *me*?

MR HADID. Yes.

KELLY. Sorry. We're confused.

MR HADID. The shoes on your feet.

CLAY (*laughs*). Yeah?

MR HADID. Do you know how much you pay for them?

KELLY. *His* shoes.

MR HADID. I very much admire this style of shoe.

KELLY. Ohhh.

CLAY (*relieved*). Oh. Uhh . . . uhh . . . Wow. God, let me think. (*To* KELLY.) Do you . . . ?

KELLY. They're from that place.

MR HADID. They were expensive?

CLAY. Oh . . . uhh . . . well, except we usually wait for everything to go on sale.

KELLY. I'm one of those people with like a bargain *obsession*.

CLAY. So probably less than you think.

MR HADID. But do you know how much? In dollars?

CLAY. Uhhhh . . . gosh. (*To* KELLY.) Do you . . . ?

KELLY. Uhh . . . no, I don't . . . I . . . hmm. No.

CLAY. Really can't . . . uh, they're definitely comfortable.

MR HADID (*politely*). I am sorry.

CLAY. No, no.

KELLY. We could possibly find out.

MR HADID. At a more convenient time.

KELLY. We don't really keep those kind of receipts.

MR HADID. No, no. Please go on.

Back to the previous moment: lights, music, etc.

KELLY (*brandishing the avocado*). So, at the *moment*? Whether or not you're reasonable? That actually isn't the *topic* right now.

CASH. Hey, Clay.

> KELLY *exits to kitchen.*

Lemme take a look at your kid.

CLAY (*to* CASH). *Shhh* . . . could you? A little? Do you mind?

CASH (*re.* KELLY). She's not paying attention.

CLAY. I know. Just. Try to.

> CLAY *turns down the music.*

CASH. What's the big deal?

CLAY. It's not a big deal.

CASH. Not a big deal to *me*.

CLAY. Me either.

CASH. Happy to.

CLAY. Thanks.

CASH. Just tell me when.

CLAY. Not yet, but –

CASH. Awaiting your signal.

CLAY. Maybe when they come upstairs.

CASH. Standing by, chief.

Pause.

CLAY. I mean, I just don't want it to *seem* like a big deal.

CASH. What, you mean to your *wife*?

CLAY. No.

CASH. I'm not gonna say anything.

CLAY. I know.

CASH. To Mom?

CLAY. No, I just –

CASH. I'm discreet.

CLAY. I mean to Kayla.

CASH. She scared of me?

CLAY. No.

CASH. You told her who I am?

CLAY. Yeah.

CASH. You said this is Uncle Cash?

CLAY. Yeah.

CASH. So how am I making it a big deal?

CLAY. You know how.

CASH. I do?

CLAY. Yes, you do.

CASH. I'm not sure I do.

CLAY. The way you are.

CASH. The way I am?

CLAY. The way you can be.

CASH. What way is that?

CLAY. You know.

CASH. Tell me what way.

CLAY. I think you know.

CASH. Say what you mean.

CLAY. The attitude.

CASH. *My* attitude.

CLAY. You know the attitude.

CASH. My *professional* attitude?

CLAY. General attitude.

CASH. So, my *personality.*

CLAY. And I'd prefer it if you wouldn't.

CASH. Have the attitude.

CLAY. Today, anyway.

CASH. Because of the *children.*

CLAY. Kids don't understand when you . . . I'd just prefer it.

CASH. That's your preference.

CLAY. Yes, it is.

CASH. About my attitude.

CLAY. Right.

CASH. Gracious. Well then, on behalf of the *children.*

KALINA *tiptoes through the room, hiding from* KAYLA, *a finger to her lips, and exits again.*

Sooo . . . Big *golfer* now, huh?

CLAY. For example.

CASH. Now there's a sport.

CLAY. Case in point.

CASH. The ladies *love* the golfers.

CLAY. Hm-mm.

CASH. Strolling the links in a pair of crisp white shorts.

CLAY. Hate to break this to you –

CASH. The ladies *cream* for the golfers.

CLAY. – but I'm not looking for your approval.

CASH. Not a dry panty in the clubhouse.

CLAY. Hey, you know what? Forget it.

CASH. Why?

CLAY. If this is how it's gonna be.

CASH. How what is?

CLAY. Big surprise.

CASH. What did I do?

CLAY. So it's going to be like this?

CASH. Like what?

CLAY. That's your choice? Years can go by, but *still*.

CASH. What's it like?

CLAY. Like this. Like unpleasant.

CASH. I don't find you unpleasant.

CLAY. Yeah, yeah, yeah.

CASH. Ohhh, you mean *me*.

CLAY. Never changes.

CASH. But I'm making *pleasantries*.

CLAY. Yeah. Right. Uhhh . . . here's a thought: *kiss my ass*?

CASH. Well, *that* was unpleasant.

CLAY. I'll take her to the pediatrician, you know? Thought you wouldn't mind.

CASH. I don't mind.

CLAY. If I ask every once in a very rare while for a favour –

CASH. So not only do you want me to do your kid this medical favour but I also have to maintain a certain *attitude* –

CLAY. So you *do* mind.

CASH. A favour for which, by the way, most people would make an *appointment*.

CLAY. So don't say you don't mind when clearly you –

CASH. For which most people would *pay* –

CLAY. You might have warned me you were planning to be like this.

CASH. You might have warned me that you were still a little fascist.

CLAY (*seeing* CAROL *and* KELLY). Shhh.

CAROL *and* KELLY *enter, carrying place settings.*

KELLY . . . and I'm stranded there on the runway in *Orange County*. At *John Wayne Airport*, which I think says it all, and I'm talking to this young white man next to me who is headed to West Africa to do his *missionary work* like *trick or treat* for the Republican Party . . .

KAYLA *has entered, searching for* KALINA. *She has one hand inside her pull-up. She exits again.*

Clay, did you put her in a pull-up?

CLAY. Yes, I did.

KELLY. Why is she scratching like that?

CAROL (*re. table settings*). Which way does this go, now?

KELLY. I'll do it. And this man opens his bag – and remember I'm actually *conversing* with this person – opens his carry-on and it is filled, top to bottom, with *Bibles*, *American flags* and laminated pictures of our *president*.

CAROL. Oh. Thank God, only two more years of that little smirking face.

KELLY. And I'm thinking *how dare you*, you TGI Fridays customer. You TJ Maxx shopper with your iceberg lettuce and your ranch dressing and the right to vote. *How dare you*. I mean the *audacity*.

KAYLA *and* KALINA *run through screaming again, this time in the other direction.*

KALINA (*as they pass through*). I cannot catch her! She is too fast for me! Is crazy fast girl!

CLAY (*upon seeing them*). Sweetie? C'mere a second.

KELLY. And I'm sorry, Carol, I'm all for inclusion. But that part of the country? Those are not my people.

KELLY *and* CAROL *have exited to the kitchen again. Pause.*

CASH. Shouldn't leave food lying around.

CLAY. What food?

CASH. Why ya got that rodent problem.

CLAY. We don't leave food lying around.

CASH. Mom said you got a maid.

CLAY. Cleaning person. Yes.

CASH. Maybe pay her a little more.

CLAY. We pay her very well.

CASH. To make sure there's no food lying around.

CLAY. There isn't.

CASH (*shrugs*). *Avocados*, you said.

CLAY. Where do you suggest they ripen?

CASH. She's foreign, right?

CLAY. Who?

CASH. Maid. Foreigner?

CLAY. You have a problem with that?

CASH. Probably wants more money.

CLAY. We pay her very well.

CASH. It's why she came here, right? Make money?

CLAY. We give her lunch. We give her a room to put her stuff in.

CASH. Mom says she steals.

CLAY. *What?!*

KALINA *appears on the stairs.*

KALINA. Cash, come look with me at the baby sleeping!

CLAY. Mom's out of her fucking mind.

KALINA (*rapturously*). Oh God! He is so cute when lying like this in the sleeping position!

CASH (*to* CLAY, *ignoring* KALINA). What happened to your cat?

KALINA (*joining them*). This is what I want is the babies! To be married and have my stomach filled with the big babies and feeling the kicks!

CASH. What happened to Chester?

KALINA. Cash!! Come to look!

CASH. Had a cat, you wouldn't have a rodent problem.

KALINA (*to* CASH). Aaaargh! (*To* CLAY.) He is so boring, your brother! He always like to do nothing. And so I never do anything also. Yesterday I say to him, hey, I say why we not sometime go dancing? He says – (*Imitating him.*) I'm not a *faggot*. I say, *Cash*. Don't be stupid. Is sexy to dance, you know? Does not make you the faggot to be liking to dance! And on top of the things, is way to have fun and meet the people. He say why do I want to meet the people? I say, uhh, because *you are human being*? I say I wish that I can go and meet the faggots because I believe the faggots are having more of the fun than *you*! (*To* CASH.) Oh, hee hee, ha ha. Go and be with the laughing. You are fucked over, you know?

CASH. Up.

KALINA (*to* CLAY). Is totally fucked over to be thinking like this, yes?

CASH. The preposition you are looking for is *up*.

KALINA (*to* CASH). Hey. Excuse me. I know fucked over. Okay? Is expression.

CASH (*laughs, quietly*). Whatever. Fuckin' nitwit.

KALINA. What do you call me?

CASH (*laughing*). Fucked over.

KALINA. Excuse me, what do you call me now?

CASH (*to himself*). I take it back. I *am* fucked over.

KALINA. I know this word, Cash. The word *nitwit*. Do not be calling me the names in front of your family, all right? Do you hear? Is not right, you know?

MR HADID, *standing by the dining table, interrupts again. Lights change.*

MR HADID. Excuse me once again.

CLAY. Hmm?

MR HADID. I am wondering about the table.

CLAY. Yeah?

MR HADID. This one.

CLAY. Yeah?

MR HADID. Very nice.

CLAY. Oh, thanks.

MR HADID. Very good table.

CLAY. Parsons table, yeah.

MR HADID. And you could fix it.

CLAY. Fix what?

MR HADID. The table. It is easy to fix. If you were to use the sandpaper? To rub it with the sandpaper. And you fill in these little holes. Here. And here. And then you use the beeswax. In this way, you bring out the pattern of the grain.

CLAY. Well. But. You know. It's *distressed*.

MR HADID. But you could fix it.

CLAY. No, I mean, it's *supposed* to look like that.

MR HADID. Ahh.

CLAY. It's *made* that way.

MR HADID (*smiles*). Ahh. And do you know how much you pay for it?

CLAY (*reluctant*). Oh. Uhh . . . gosh.

MR HADID. It was expensive?

CLAY. Interestingly, not as much as the chairs.

MR HADID. But can you say how much? In dollars.

CLAY. The thing is . . . The thing is, maybe we should talk about that *later*.

MR HADID. Forgive me.

CLAY. No no no. It's fine. It's just we're trying to talk about *one* thing and then . . .

MR HADID. None of my *beeswax*.

CLAY. No, no, no, no.

MR HADID. And I have interrupted.

CLAY. You're our *guest*. Please.

MR HADID. I will be more careful.

CLAY. Can I get you anything else? Something to eat?

MR HADID. Please. Continue.

The previous scene resumes.

KALINA. I know this word, Cash. The word *nitwit*. Do not be calling me the names in front of your family, all right? Do you hear? Is not right, you know?

KAYLA has re-entered, looking for KALINA. CASH is chuckling.

Oh, big funny joke. How we are laughing now.

CLAY (*quietly, to* KAYLA). Sweetie, don't scratch, okay? You just make it worse.

CASH (*to* KAYLA). Hey. C'mere a second.

He checks with CLAY, *who silently indicates for* CASH *to proceed. As* KALINA *talks,* CASH *leads* KAYLA *by the hand out of the room.*

KALINA (*to* CLAY). Ohhh, you know, last month we are going to New York? Cash and I are going to New York and we go to the Ground Zero and it is so *sad*, you know? To think how all the people die? And is still just big empty hole sitting there with nothing? *So sad.* Do you ever go to New York to see the Ground Zero?

CLAY. No.

KALINA. Is good to go there, so maybe you will.

CLAY. Maybe.

KALINA. For the nation.

CLAY. Maybe we will.

KALINA. And I buy these *boots* there, too!

CLAY. Those are great.

KALINA. I spend so much *money*! But still is good because is hard to find good shoes sometime.

CLAY. Uh, how long have you been in the US?

KALINA. Four and half years. Oh, hey! You know what it is I am thinking? In place where I am little girl, in village? We have the *weasels*, you know? And always they are getting into the places where there is the food? And I am also thinking maybe the weasels are in this place.

CLAY. It's possible.

KALINA. Is so weird! I say to Cash, you have *brother* here and you not ever see him? Is *wrong*, you know? Because your *family*, this is the people who would *kill* for you. And you for them.

CLAY. Right.

KALINA. But you are so lucky to have Kelly, who make so much money so that you can do *nothing* all day but to be the perfect father for the children? So lucky for you!!

CASH *re-enters with* KAYLA *as* CAROL *and* KELLY *enter with place settings.* CASH *continues into kitchen.*

KELLY . . . *in* which, of course, corporate media is totally complicit, since if you decide you're going to *hurt* people, as our president seems *determined* to do, then of course it helps to *vilify* them in advance so that we don't have to *feel so bad* when we start dropping bombs on them. Oh, uhh –

KALINA *is lighting a cigarette.*

(*To* KALINA.) Wait. Wait. Excuse me? (*To* CLAY.) Hello?

CLAY. Oh, yeah. We don't . . . in the house, generally –

KALINA. Ohh yes! I forget, Kelly! It is so true!

CAROL (*re. place settings*). Oh, look. I'm doing everything backwards, aren't I?

KELLY. I'll do it. You sit.

KALINA. Hey, Kayla! You go with me while I do the smoking! (*To* CLAY). Is okay, yes?

CLAY *looks to* KELLY.

CLAY. Umm . . . actually . . . ?

KALINA (*understanding*). Ohh, I see it now. I am to show bad example. Is okay. Hey, Kayla! See how I am doing the smoking? This is sooo bad, so don't do it when you are bigger. Even if it make you look sexy and things? Don't do it.

KELLY. Clay, are you going to open that bottle of wine?

KALINA (*as she exits*). Don't ever to be like me.

CLAY. Mom? Glass of wine?

CLAY *exits to kitchen.* KAYLA *tugs at* KELLY*'s leg as she sets the table.*

CAROL. I get so confused lately. I start to worry that I could have some of the *warning signs*.

KELLY (*to* KAYLA). Not now, sweetie.

CAROL. Do you know that joke about the woman whose doctor says to her I have some terrible news for you, Mrs Jones, he says, I'm afraid you have Alzheimer's Disease? And then the doctor says . . . (*Confused.*) Oh, no, wait. Oh, *poop*.

KELLY (*calling to the kitchen*). Clay, can you also bring the candles?

CAROL. No, see . . . now I have it all wrong.

CLAY (*from off*). They're on the table.

KELLY. No they're not. (*To* CAROL.) I'm listening. The doctor says you have Alzheimer's.

CAROL. Oh! Oh! Now I remember. This is it. He says you have *cancer.*

KELLY. Ah. Very different.

CAROL. The doctor in the *joke*. He says, you have incurable *cancer*. You have to say that part first.

KELLY (*to* KAYLA). Sweetie-pie, please? (*To* CAROL.) Right. So the doctor says, you have *cancer.*

CAROL. He says you have incurable cancer, and the woman says, oh, how terrible, and *then* the doctor says, but, you see, it's even *worse* than that –

KELLY (*smiles, knowing the punchline*). Ohhh. Right, right. Okay, I get it now.

CAROL. Oh, you've *heard* it.

KELLY. Uhhh . . . he says it's worse than that, you also have Alzheimer's, and she says, oh, thank God, I thought you were going to tell me I had cancer.

CAROL. Now see, that just makes me laugh.

KELLY (*to* KAYLA, *finally*). What, sweetie? Use your words.

KELLY *bends down and* KAYLA *whispers in her ear as* CLAY *enters from the kitchen with the bottle of wine.*

CAROL. Isn't it odd, Clay? Both Charlton Heston *and* Ronald Reagan. With the Alzheimer's? Isn't that a coincidence? Both actors. And both Republicans.

CLAY. Oh, right. Well. Fuck 'em.

CAROL. Well, *precisely.*

KELLY (*taking* KAYLA *toward the stairs*). Okay, sweetie. Mommy's gonna change your Huggie then you can help me set the table.

CLAY. No, no, no, no, no! What do you mean? What are you . . . ? I just put one on her.

KELLY. She says she's itchy.

CLAY (*to* KAYLA). Sweetie, Daddy just gave you a brand new Huggie, remember? We don't need another Huggie.

CAROL (*with concern*). Ohhh, is Kayla wearing her little Huggie?

CLAY. Mom, can we not make her self-conscious, okay?

KELLY. Clay, she's not comfortable.

CLAY. Well, that's not the point, is it? (*To* KAYLA.) See, sweetie, the Huggies aren't just *free*, you know, the Huggies cost *money*.

KELLY. For Christ's *sake*, Clay.

CAROL (*to* KAYLA). I know some big girls who wear *grown-up* pants because *their* mommies and daddies

CLAY. Mom? Why don't you just relax?

KELLY. Maybe we could *all* relax.

CLAY (*to* KELLY). Well, who deals with this every single day, huh? Is it you? Or is it me?

KELLY. Fine. Let her scratch.

CLAY (*to* KAYLA). Daddy's the Huggie-changer, right, pumpkin? We don't need to bother Mommy.

KALINA *returns from outside*.

KALINA (*to* KAYLA). I know what it is that is wrong with Kayla. Yes I do. She need to be *teekled!* And I am coming to get her and teekle her!!

KAYLA *shrieks and races away,* KALINA *following.*

(*Exiting.*) Stop! I command you to stop for my teekling!!

CAROL *sits by* MR HADID. CLAY *turns to him. Lights change.*

CLAY. See, I feel sorry for people out there. These people without kids. And I hate to use the cliché, it sounds like such a cliché, but it's a *gift*, right? To be able to, with your kids, to recapture some of . . . our . . . *innocence*. Get some of that back. Reconnect with the innocence. Because if you *don't*, then, you know? Then it . . . it . . . it's *lost*. It *collapses*, like, like, like . . .

MR HADID. Like a soufflé.

CAROL (*to* MR HADID). Ohhh, do you know the word 'soufflé'?

MR HADID. Of course, yes.

CLAY (*re. his glass*). Did you want more of that, or . . . ?

MR HADID. Yes, please. Thank you.

CLAY *takes his glass and exits.*

CAROL. Loss is so difficult.

MR HADID. Yes.

CAROL. How old was she?

MR HADID. She was forty-two.

CAROL. And you have a son?

MR HADID. One son, yes, ma'am.

CAROL. Let me ask you something. I was watching a documentary the other night on PBS. I don't know if you watch PBS. I'm a subscriber. And sometimes I volunteer for the pledge drives. But mostly I think, what else is there to watch? I mean, really, well, there's the Discovery Channel.

But ninety-nine per cent of what's on television I just look
at it and I . . . I don't disapprove, I mean, more power to all
that. Diversity and everything. Diversity is so important.
But it's like with junk food, isn't it? I say to my first-
graders, if all you eat is junk food, then you can hardly
expect to feel good about yourself. And you know, I was
showing them a wonderful programme all about families
around the world, from each continent, and when they got
to some tribesmen in New Guinea, who wear very little
clothing, just some leaves and . . . gourds, but it's the
tropics, after all, well, some of the children started to laugh.
And, you know, that just upset me so much. So I said to
them, well now, let's all just think for a minute. Let's think
how you would like to be laughed at. If you went to New
Guinea right now, dressed in your American clothes? That
wouldn't be very nice, would it? How do we ever expect to
reach out to new cultures and embrace new ideas if all we
can do is laugh? (*Back to her main point.*) And plus, Bill
Moyers is so wonderful. So I was watching the documentary,
which was all about Genghis Khan. Did you see that?

MR HADID. I don't think so.

KAYLA *has approached* CAROL. *She holds one hand
behind her back.*

CAROL. Well, look who's here now. Do you want to say
hello? Do you want to do that? Hmm?

KAYLA *shakes her head.*

Oh, oh now, wait. Is that a surprise? Maybe let's not. Okay?
Because remember how some surprises aren't so nice?
Remember? So only if it's a nice sur –

KAYLA *produces a screwdriver.* CAROL *flinches.*

Ohhh. All right. Well, that's a nice thing. I like screwdrivers.
Screwdrivers are useful. Thank you. This will be *very useful.*

KAYLA *exits.*

I'm sorry. *How* old was she, did you say?

MR HADID. Forty-two.

CAROL. She had diabetes?

MR HADID. Yes, ma'am.

CAROL. What a terrible way to . . .

MR HADID. Yes, ma'am.

CAROL. You see, because we don't *listen* to each other. We
   don't. My husband, for example. He was not a good listener.
   But the lovely thing about *Eastern* wisdom, *I* think, what
   we learn from . . . from the . . . wait, where are the monks
   from? Oh, you know, the monks. The country with the
   meditation. The Asian country.

MR HADID. China?

CAROL. No, no, no, smaller.

MR HADID. Korea?

CAROL. No, but landlocked.

MR HADID. Nepal?

CAROL. Oh, what is wrong with me? No, from our meditation
   class. More to the West.

MR HADID. Bhutan?

CAROL. And it's mountainous. With the yaks, you know. The
   yaks and the political problems?

MR HADID. Mongol – ?

CAROL. *Tibet!* Thank you. Tibet. With the Dalai Lama. The
   Tibetan monks. And what we learn from them is, it seems to
   me, it's the value of *listening*.

Pause. MR HADID *nods.*

Tell me again, *how* old was she?

KAYLA *and* KALINA *dash in, using Nerf bats as guns to
   shoot at each other.* KAYLA *is shrieking. Music returns.*

KALINA (*makes shooting sounds*). Ahhh! No! The bullets they are hitting her but still she lives!! She is *Supergirl*! Nooo! She shoots me! Arrrgghhh!!

CLAY *enters from the kitchen. He is wearing an apron and oven mitts.*

CLAY (*interrupting*). Hey. Sorry. Sweetie? No shooting, okay? Let's not shoot.

KALINA. Is okay. Is no real bullets.

CLAY. It's just we don't do shooting games.

KALINA. Oh, yes.

CLAY. Not to be all preachy about it.

KALINA. Nooo, is true. With the guns being so bad in the nation.

CLAY (*to* KAYLA). But you're having some fun, aren't you, huh? Aren't you, Special K?

CAROL. Clay, did you know this? That Charlton Heston wears a *toupee*?

KALINA (*to* KAYLA). Hey! I know! Now I am to swordfight with you! (*En garde.*) Ha-haaa!

They begin fencing.

CLAY. Wait. Sorry. Kalina? Uhhh . . . martial arts? Guns. It's all the emphasis on *conflict*?

KALINA (*stopping*). Ohhh, yes.

CAROL. And *John Wayne*, too. A toupee. And one doesn't normally think of him as *vain*. Now, someone told me that *he* did a movie about Genghis Khan. Now that's just silly. That's *miscasting*.

KELLY *has entered with a centrepiece.*

KALINA (*to* KELLY, *who ignores her*). Oh, Kelly! So pretty! Look at table! Is she so perfect or what?!

CAROL. Now, tell me the one who played Gandhi.

KELLY. Ben Kingsley.

CAROL. No, that's not it.

KELLY. It was Ben Kingsley.

CAROL. No, I don't think so. I think he was Indian.

KELLY. Ben Kingsley is English.

CAROL. No, this actor is olive-skinned.

CLAY. Ben. Kingsley.

KELLY *continues upstairs as* CASH *returns with a martini.*

CAROL. Well, I don't think you're right, but anyway, the English actors are just *better.* Don't you think? Especially in historical films. You can't have American actors playing those parts, it never *sounds* right. Wait, now, who is the one from that movie about the Conquistadors?

CLAY (*on his way back to kitchen*). Uhhh . . . I don't know.

CAROL. And I think he also was in *Dr Zhivago.*

CLAY. I don't know.

CAROL. Oh, yes you do. Of course you do. You know.

CLAY (*calling from the kitchen*). I don't know.

CAROL (*to* KALINA). Well, I don't really go to the *commercial* sort of movies anyway. I suppose it's all the talking in the audience. Although I know that people in certain communities enjoy that, all the talking, and I don't want to discourage that if it's their *custom.* Now, where I live we have a university cinema. They show the smaller movies, and those I like.

CASH (*to himself, opening a magazine*). The ones black people don't go to.

CLAY *returns with bottle and glasses as* KELLY *returns from upstairs with the* BABY.

CLAY. Anybody? Glass of wine before we eat?

KALINA. Ohhh, yes please for me, thank you.

CASH. Oughta go to porn films, Mom. People don't talk during those.

CAROL. I have no objection to pornography.

CASH. Although they do *moan* from time to time.

CAROL. We do have a thing called the First Amendment.

KELLY. Right, but Carol –

CAROL. In fact, we knew a couple that had quite an extensive collection of pornography.

CLAY. Who?

CAROL. The Teverbaughs.

CLAY. Dr Teverbaugh.

CAROL. That's right.

CLAY. Pornography?

CAROL. It was their interest.

CLAY. My orthodontist.

CASH. I *thought* his fingers tasted funny.

CAROL. It can be a marital aid. If the couple has the shared interest, it can help the marriage.

CASH. But then it's not *porn*. How can that be *porn*?

CLAY (*looking at the ceiling*). Shh, shh. Hey, you guys?

CASH. You can't look at porn with your *wife*. That's the moment it ceases to function as *porn*.

CLAY. Hey. Shhh. Shhh.

KALINA. Is not *sexy*, though. This is the problem. The porn, you know, is just not *sexy*.

CLAY. *Shhh!!* Shut up. Shut up.

CAROL. Oh, don't say *shut up*.

All stop. CLAY *turns off the music and stares at the ceiling.*

KELLY. What?

CAROL. What?

CLAY. Did you hear that?

CASH. What?

CAROL. What?

CLAY. Shhh. Listen.

They do.

You didn't hear that?

KELLY. No.

KALINA. Where are we hearing?

CLAY. Up on the roof.

CAROL (*to* KAYLA). Maybe Santa came *early*!

CLAY. Shhh!!

They listen. Nothing.

No one heard that?

All mumble 'No'.

Never mind.

KALINA. Because, you know, I have in the past the boyfriend who was in the porns? And he says you know is all just faking! Is not their real *feelings*, you know? And also the bright lights and the fat peoples. Is not sexy.

CAROL. Still, people should be free to choose.

KALINA. Okay sure, is fine if you like to look at the fat peoples. I like much more the romantic love scenes. These to me are the more sexy.

CASH. I always watch *The Bridges of Madison County* when I want to ejaculate.

KELLY. Okay, but Carol. While I can agree with you that there may be this theoretical household where pornography is *shared* as a quote unquote *marital tool*, isn't the porn collection far more likely to be the private hobby of *one particular* partner? And how exactly does *that* aid the marital situation?

CAROL. You may be right.

CASH (*reading, not looking up*). I could beat off to the *Reader's Digest*.

KELLY. Not to belabour the topic.

CAROL. I don't mind the topic.

KELLY. But it's different when children are involved.

CAROL (*amused*). Though it may not be the ideal topic for a holiday established by Puritans.

KALINA. Is weird holiday, you know? Where we all eat of the same bird which then makes us feel sleepy.

CAROL (*happy to change the subject*). Well, someday let's all celebrate a holiday in your country!

KALINA. Ecch. Why? Oh, no, Carol. Is stupid place. Is nothing to do. Is just old men who piss in street all of the time. And the cars too expensive for the people. America is much better for living. Here *everyone* have the cars. Even the poor black people have the car. Why do the black people get the cars? They have no *money*. Get cars with the credit cards. Credit cards good deal for the black people. And they just *send* to them in the *mail*! Send them the credit card and say here, black people, go buy the car with this!

CAROL (*reinterpreting positively*). Corporations *do* prey on the disadvantaged. That is so true.

KALINA. Mmm, this wine is so delicious, the taste of it!

CAROL (*to* KALINA). But see, it's just, that's the thing about PBS, I always think, how it gives you a broader perspective on the different cultures. You know, Clay has the cleaning lady that always wears the scarf on her head? And I said to her your scarf is so *pretty*, did you bring that from your country?

CLAY. Yeah. Hey, Mom?

CAROL. Although I'm not sure she understood me. (*To* CLAY.) Hmm?

CLAY. Did you accuse her of *stealing*?

CAROL. *What?!* I *never* . . . No!

CLAY. That's what Cash says.

CAROL. *Absolutely not!* I would *never* in a million –

CASH (*overlapping*). What you said to me.

CAROL (*continuing*). – *years*! Oh, *stop it*. I didn't say that *at all*. I would *never*.

CASH. What you said was in her bag.

CAROL. Oh, that is *offensive*. All I said was the *bread*. She had the *bread*.

CLAY. When?

CAROL. But I would never *accuse* a person to their fa – I didn't say anything to *her*.

KELLY. What bread?

CAROL. You know, that bread that you get with the nuts in it. I just saw her *bag*, but it was only *half* of the loaf, and I certainly never *accused* anyone.

CLAY. Well, *Mom*. Whatever you saw –

CAROL. I was looking for the fabric softener sheets and I went in that back room where she keeps her things –

CLAY. But *so what*?! Even if she *did*. It's *bread*.

CAROL. I'm *agreeing* with you. My goodness.

CLAY. Let her take anything she wants.

CAROL. That's what I'm *saying*! Of course it's *nothing*! When you stop and think of everything we *have*.

KELLY. Are you talking about the *fig* bread?

CAROL. With the figs and the nuts.

KELLY. There's a whole loaf of that in the breadbox.

CAROL. When you think of the *abundance*. It's almost shameful that anyone in the world would ever go *hungry*.

CASH. I'm hungry right now.

CAROL. That is exactly why I always support the Workers' Party candidates.

KELLY. Well, Carol. I mean, forgive me, but *really*.

CAROL. I'm making a statement.

CLAY. Yeah, the statement is I flush my vote down the toilet.

CAROL. The Socialist Workers' Party is hardly down the *toilet*.

KALINA. *Socialist??!!*

CAROL. I like to *believe* in what I vote for, not calculate between the lesser of . . .

KALINA (*to* KAYLA, *laughing hard*). She says she is socialist!

CAROL (*calmly*). Well, my husband wasn't a *dedicated* socialist –

KALINA. Here?!

CAROL. But I think that history will show, in the long run –

KELLY. Well, sure, if you're talking *economically*, if you mean following the Scandinavian model.

KALINA (*realising they are serious*). Excuse me now? But are you crazy?!

The BABY *starts to cry.*

KELLY (*to* BABY). Shhhh. Okay. Okay.

KALINA. Are you completely insane people?! Because I have to tell you this is how you are sounding!!

CASH. Can we go back to talking about porn?

KALINA. I'm sorry, but this is craziest thing that you say!

KELLY *opens the front of her shirt to allow the* BABY *to nurse.*

KELLY (*to* BABY). Shhh, shhh . . .

CAROL. The point is, if *we* have so much, shouldn't there be a *system* so that everyone can have bread *all* of the time? Then *no one* has to steal.

CLAY. Mom! No one stole any bread!

CAROL. Don't be argumentative! I'm *saying* I want to *give* them bread.

KALINA. Why *give* them? The people can get the jobs!

CASH. Fuckin' A.

KALINA. *I* have job! I *pay* for the bread! Is no one going to give *me* bread!

CAROL. Then at least the skills so that they can make their *own* bread.

KALINA. To be lazy and do nothing like the blacks and the Mexicans does not mean *I* have to give them the bread! The lazy people do not for nothing get my bread!

CLAY (*peacemaker*). Okay. Okay. Okay.

CAROL. But we *like* to give! It's *blessed* to give.

KELLY (*condescendingly, to* KALINA, *as the* BABY *nurses*). Well, excuse me. Listen . . . I . . . the obvious point *is* . . . Sorry what's your *name*?

KALINA. It is Kalina.

CASH (*to* KALINA). She knows your name.

KELLY. Right. I think the point is, I *hope*? That the accumulated wisdom of your nineteen years might not be all that comprehensive, okay?

CASH (*overlapping*). She's twenty-three.

KELLY (*continuing*). And that there might be some value in not *shouting* at people who actually read the paper and keep up with world affairs.

KALINA. Okay, and what I am saying to you now, Kelly? Because you are so much smarter and things? What I am saying is I don't understand all the words that you say.

CASH (*to* KALINA). She's trying to insult you.

KALINA (*ignoring* CASH). What is the word 'coomolated'?

CASH. No, no, no, no, no. Look. (*To* KALINA.) First of all. See, in this country, some of the rich people, you see, they feel *verrry guilty*.

CLAY. *Rich?* You call this *rich*?

CAROL. Oh, let's let it drop.

CASH. They feel so *frivolous*. They feel *ashamed*.

CLAY. This isn't rich. Trust me, I can show you *rich*.

CASH. They think, *oh no, people are starving*, and they can't *enjoy* how rich they are because they feel so *tacky*.

CLAY. This is why you finally come to our house? To pass *judgement* on us?

CASH. They say, *if we were really good people we'd give eeeverything away*.

CLAY. So don't come next time.

CASH. But the truth is, they don't *really* want to give away their stuff. Their golf clubs and their fifty-two-inch TV. Not to some starving illiterate natives in some desert somewhere. Not *really*.

CLAY. Whose car gets eight miles to the gallon, Cash? Huh? Not *ours*!

CAROL. Why don't we play a game? What's the name of that game we played?

CASH. See, they *feel* bad because what they practise doesn't square with what they preach. Which makes them every bit as bad as the materialistic barbarians they despise!

CLAY *laughs derisively.*

CAROL. What's that game where you draw the little pictures?

CASH. And you want to say to these people: hey, you don't have to change what you *practise*. That's way too *hard*. Just change what you fucking *preach*.

CLAY. Oh, fuck *you*. Up on your mountain top.

CAROL (*clapping hands like a schoolteacher*). All right! We're all going to change the subject right now!

KELLY. How lovely to see your brother again, Clay. I've missed him so much.

CLAY. You don't speak for us, okay? Don't presume to speak for us.

Then KELLY*'s nipple is bitten.*

KELLY. *Oww!!* Jesus. *Fucking teeth.*

She stands and exits upstairs, with the now crying BABY. *Pause.*

CAROL. You know what movie I *did* enjoy. The one . . . oh, you know the one. It's Italian. And there's a very funny man in it. And it's during the Holocaust. Not that I have to have a happy ending. But I do like to feel that I'm a better person for having watched it.

CASH. And you don't get that from porn?

KAYLA *turns on a loud, bright cartoon.*

CLAY. *Sweetie? Pumpkin?*

CAROL (*to* KAYLA). Oh! What is *that*? *Hmm?* Doesn't that look *fun*! I want to watch that with *Kayla*!

KALINA (*to* CASH). You don't want the wine? It is so delicious!

CASH *waves her away.*

CLAY (*to* KAYLA). Okay, but not too loud. Okay, sweetie?

KALINA *joins* KAYLA *and* CAROL. CLAY, *gingerly, sits next to* CASH.

So . . . you got to . . . you got a look at it?

CASH. Your kid, you mean?

CLAY. Yeah, her . . . her . . . you know, her . . . (*He points to his genitals.*)

CASII. Yeah. I can give her something for that.

CLAY. That'd be great. Thanks.

CASH *pulls out a prescription pad.*

CASH. What's today, the twenty-sixth?

CLAY. Twenty-seventh. So, what? So, like a pill?

CASH. Ointment.

CLAY. It's just so red and inflamed. Down there. You know?

CASH. Yeah.

CLAY. Been that way a couple of days.

CASH. Looks painful, yeah.

CLAY. Ever seen anything like that before?

CASH. Uhhh . . . dunno.

CLAY. All . . . *scaly*. And there's this . . . this . . . sticky . . .

CASH. Discharge. Yeah. This'll stop her scratching it.

CASH *begins writing.*

CLAY. We're really happy you came.

CASH. Mmm.

CLAY. Good for kids to see their family.

CASH. They don't see their family?

CLAY. Extended family.

CASH (*as he writes*). So use this twice a day. Like before she goes to sleep and then again in the morning. Just the ulcerated area around the outer part of the vulva. And around the anus, too, you know, if she starts scratching back there.

CLAY. Okay. Not just me. Kelly too. I'm sure she is.

CASH. Mm-hmm.

CLAY. Always seemed like you guys had a lot in common.

CASH *nods*.

And you know, whatever you might think, you really don't know her. You don't. She's a complicated person who's been through a lot, and I know you don't care or possibly even *recall*? But a few years ago? Before we had Kayla? She was going through some difficult stuff, but we got through it, you know, we got past it, and one of the things I came away with is an understanding of what an amazing person she is.

CASH *tears off and hands* CLAY *the prescription*.

CASH. So just take that to any pharmacy.

CLAY. Right. And that'll clear it up.

CASH. The sores . . . little blisters. Should, yeah.

CLAY. And you think it has to do with fleas? Or lice? From something getting in the house?

CASH. Could be.

CLAY. Don't you think?

CASH. Could be that.

CLAY. Since they carry all those diseases.

CASH. Could be any number of things.

CLAY *stares.*

CLAY. Well, is this the right medicine or not?

CASH. It's *medicinal.*

CLAY. Meaning *what*? Meaning it'll *cure* it?

CASH. Depends on what you mean by cure.

CLAY. Well, *what does she have*, Cash? (*Drops his voice.*) Huh? Don't fuck around with me.

CASH. What do you want me to say? I'm a *plastic surgeon*, all right? I dunno everything.

CLAY. But what's with the *attitude*? Huh? You think this is *funny*? Or *ironic*, or something?

CASH. Although the word *anus* is funny.

CLAY. Go ahead and smirk at *me*. I don't care.

CASH (*snickering*). Anus.

CLAY. But to amuse yourself at the expense of a *child*?

CASH. Hey. Take your nerve tonic, *Aunt Polly.*

CLAY. Just because some of us are trying to do something a little less *cowardly.*

CASH. Look. Do me a favour.

CLAY. A little less *selfish.*

CASH. Go talk to your *wife*, all right? Because, honestly?

CLAY. *Wait, wait, wait, wait, wait, shhhh!* (*To the others, re. TV.*) Turn that off.

CAROL. What's the matter? Why are you shout – ?

CLAY. *Off, please! Can we please turn that off?!*

CLAY *grabs remote, turns off the TV.*

KALINA (*to* CLAY). What is problem?

CLAY. I'm saying everybody please be quiet.

KELLY *has entered from kitchen.*

KELLY. What happened?

CLAY (*staring at the ceiling*). Shhh!! Shut up, shut up!!

KELLY. What are you doing?

CLAY. Could we all be quiet and *listen*? Could we do that, please?

Pause. All is silent.

You're telling me you didn't hear that?

All reply: 'What?' 'No.' 'Hear what?', etc.

No one heard that? You are seriously *kidding* me.

KALINA. I still don't know for what is we are listening.

CLAY. There was movement. No one else heard some sort of overhead movement? Am I the only one who cares?

CAROL. All *right*.

CLAY. Apparently so.

CAROL. We're all listening.

CLAY. Apparently I am.

KELLY. Have a *spasm*, that helps.

CAROL. Shhh. Everyone. Quiet now.

All look up at the ceiling. They wait. In the middle of the silence:

CASH. AHHH!! LOOK OUT!!

Everyone jumps. CASH *cracks up.*

Then, KAYLA *screams.*

CAROL.	CLAY.	KELLY.	KALINA.
Oh, Cash,	Hysterically	Wow. Really	See? This is
really. For	funny. Try	sophisticated.	what he is like.
heaven's sake,	growing up	It's such a	Is so stupid
don't *do* that.	for a change,	pleasure to	some of the
That is just	you cretin.	see you again,	times. Cannot
not funny.		Cash, it truly is.	believe it.

CLAY. No, no, pumpkin. Uncle Cash was just playing a yelling game.

CASH (*to* KAYLA). Let's play the yelling game.

KAYLA *screams again.*

CLAY. Sweetie. Let's not do that, okay? Serious now. (*To* CASH.) Thanks a lot.

KAYLA *does it again.* CASH *laughs.*

I want you to stop that. Daddy's not kidding, now!

CAROL (*to* KAYLA). Come here, sweetie. Let me see your dress. Look at that pretty dress you have. That's your special dress, isn't it?

KALINA (*reaching in her bag*). Hey, Kayla! How about I show you the make-up? I give you sexy makeover like the supermodel!

KELLY. Uhhh . . . I don't think . . . uh, Clay?

KALINA. Oh no, Kelly, is okay. Is my job, you know, and all the make-up is the hypoallergenics so in truth is actually being good for the skin. (*To* KAYLA.) So now you will be the hot sexy girl, yes?

KELLY. Uhh . . . yeah. Let's maybe not indoctrinate her into masculine objectification *just yet.*

KALINA *turns to* CASH *for clarification.*

KALINA. Ob-jec-dee-fi-kay?

CASH. She doesn't want her to look hot.

KALINA (*starting to apply it*). Ohhh no, Kelly. Will not be too sexy. Just only for everyday sexy look.

CLAY. But. We're saying, she is a *child*, right?

KALINA (*to* KAYLA). This is the lip-liner which we use first.

CLAY. And there's really no reason for a child to look, uhh, is there?

CAROL. Oh, Kayla! You are going to look so *pretty*!

KELLY. Okay, I really want this to stop.

CLAY. Hey, Kalina?

KALINA. I tell you what. If she don't like it, we take it off! Is easy.

CLAY. Yeah, but. But given the world we're living in. You know? With what kids are exposed to –

KALINA (*overlapping, to* KAYLA). After lining we will put in lip-colour.

CLAY (*continuing*). – wouldn't we rather protect them from certain premature experiences? Don't you think? Developmentally? Isn't that more or less obvious?

KELLY. Clay, a little less discussion, maybe.

CAROL. Even my first-graders. This is interesting. They do experience arousal. The little boys in my class? When they lie down on the sleeping mats?

CLAY. Mom?

CAROL. No. I'm not judging. I think it's sweet. I mean, they're little *men*, after all. With their little penises poking up. And the little *girls*. You can tell, when they get on the teeter-totter –

CLAY. *Mom?* Really not helping.

CASH. Ever hear the one about the paedophile at the circumcision?

CLAY. Right. That's funny.

KALINA (*to* KAYLA). Now press the lips together like this.

CLAY. To make jokes, you know, when there are sick people in the world? Sick, abusive peo – ?

CASH (*to* CLAY). Hey, I'm trying to remember. Remind me. When did you have that surgery?

CLAY. Wha . . . ?

CASH. Remember that? When they took out your sense of humour?

CAROL *cracks up.*

CLAY. Oh, right. I guess I'm crazy. Sure, everything's fine. I guess there are no more evil people in the world!!

CASH. *Evil?!*

CAROL (*laughing, to* CLAY). Oh, that's funny! That is so true about you!

CLAY. Oh, okay! Everybody relax! No more evil people! No more predators! No more child abductors!

KALINA (*to* KAYLA). Now strike pose like the supermodel!

KELLY (*to* CLAY, *re.* KALINA). Would you stop her, please?

CASH. *Evil.* What *evil*? Who are you, *Cotton Mather*?

CLAY (*to* CASH). Do you *know* the statistics? Do you *read* the paper? Or do you just prefer to talk out of your ass?

CAROL (*still laughing*). They took out his sense of humour!

CLAY. One in every five adults, Cash. One in every five. Was victimised, okay? One in every five.

CAROL. Well . . . but . . . there are five adults *here*. And nothing bad ever happened to *me*.

CLAY. Kelly was abused.

CAROL. Oh, Kelly! Ohhh.

KELLY. True.

CAROL. I didn't know that! Oh, how awful.

KELLY. The family dynamic. Yeah. Textbook case.

CAROL. Ohh, how horrible. I hope that's not true!

CLAY. It *is* true. It absolutely is.

CAROL. Ohh, I hope you can talk to someone.

KELLY. No, I do. No, it's straight out of Alice Miller. Neglect alternating with sarcasm.

CAROL (*relieved*). Ohhh! Oh, *I see*. Oh, I thought . . . oh, *p,fffft*.

CLAY. Don't be *dismissive*!

CAROL. Well, I thought she was talking about . . . *touching* things, and –

CLAY. It's *abuse*, Mom! Emotional *abuse*.

CASH. Oh, God. Not sarcasm.

CLAY. She should have been taken out of that household. *I* should have!!

CAROL. Should have *what*?

CLAY. I felt abused.

CAROL. Ohhh, *never*. I don't believe you. By who?

CLAY. Dad was *abusive*.

CASH. By *whom*? Abused by *whom*.

CAROL (*to* CLAY). Oh, *stop* it.

CLAY. Don't tell me to stop. I won't stop.

CAROL. *Abusive?*

CLAY. I won't stop. I won't. It's what I experienced.

CAROL. Nooo.

CLAY. Yes, he was. Yes, he was. Don't deny it.

CAROL. He was *irritable*, but I don't think *abusive*.

CLAY. And innocent people get hurt when *you* stick up for him and perpetuate the pattern!

CASH. Do you mean innocent as in *not guilty*?

CAROL. Well, now, wait. Now, let me think.

CASH. Or do you mean innocent like *naive*?

CAROL. No. Now, see, I would say that he was more abusive to *Cash*.

CLAY. No he wasn't! It was me!

CAROL. If it's between the two of you.

CLAY. It was *me*! This is so *unfair* of you!

CAROL (*to* CLAY). I remember him being so friendly with you.

CLAY. *Because I was seeking his approval!* Oh, this is *so* perfect. So fucking *quintessential*. Let him steal that from me, too. Just like you let him steal my Hot Wheels.

CAROL. Oh, here we go again.

CLAY. You *knew* he did it! Every single one of my Hot Wheels.

CAROL. This is so tiresome.

CASH. Mom, let Clay be abused if he wants to be.

CLAY. Remember? One day they're all *gone*. All my best ones. Disappeared! And where are they? *Surprise!* They're all hidden under his bed!

CAROL. Kicking this *same old poor dead horse*.

CLAY. As long as he denies it, sure, let him do whatever he wants! Let him steal! Just like the fucking President stole the election! *Twice*. And I bet you a thousand bucks last time he voted for the asshole. (*To* CASH.) Didn't you? Huh? A thousand bucks. Admit it. You *thief*. Come on. *Admit it*.

CASH. That's none of your business.

CLAY (*the ultimate triumph*). Ahhhahaha!! He voted for
Bush! I knew it! Look at him, Mom! For Bush! Your son
is a Republican! Your beloved little Cash is a fucking
Republican!! (*He laughs and laughs.*) Ahhhahahahahaha!!

Pause. No one knows what to say.

KALINA (*completely matter-of-fact*). But you know, Kelly,
you should put in perceptive, these things. Because when I
was raped, you know? As little girl, when I was taken to the
room and the soldiers, when they hold me down on the floor
and they rape me over and over, when I was little girl? And
then, after this, when having to have the bad abortion from
doctor which makes it now so that I cannot ever have the
children? And how I am now totally okay and everything
despite these things? And when you think how you have
family and big house and things and also the good job?
I am saying maybe is good idea to put in perceptive.

Pause.

CASH. Perspective.

KALINA (*agreeing*). Yes.

CASH. *Perspective.*

KALINA. This is what I say.

CASH. No. Per*spec*tive. The word is *perspective*.

KALINA. I *say* perceptive.

CASH. Per*speck*–tive.

CAROL. Well, *I*, for one, am getting hungry.

KALINA. Per*skep*–tive.

CASH. *Perspective!*

KALINA. Per–*skep*–

CASH. Jesus, whaddya *deaf*?

KALINA. I am trying to say the word.

CASH. *Per–speck–tive*.

KALINA. Don't yell at me.

CASH. All right. *Speck*. Say *speck*.

KALINA. Why do you yell at me?

CASH. Speck. Speck. You can't say *speck*?

KALINA. I can say it how I want to say.

CASH. Say it.

KALINA. Perskeptive.

CASH (*exploding*). PERSPECTIVE!! JESUS CHRIST, PERSPECTIVE!! PUT IT IN PERSPECTIVE!!

KALINA (*the same, overlapping*). DON'T YOU YELL AT ME, YOU FUCKING FUCKER!! YOU CANNOT YELL AT ME!!

CASH (*overlapping*). THEN LEARN SOME GODDAM ENGLISH, YOU DUMB-ASS!! HOW LONG CAN IT TAKE TO LEARN THE GODDAM ENGLISH LANGUAGE?!

KALINA (*continuous*). I AM LEAVING!! YOU STUPID ASS-MAN!! THINK YOU CAN TALK ANY WAY YOU WANT TO ME IN FRONT OF FAMILY?!

CASH. SO WHO'S STOPPING YOU, YOU LITTLE RETARD?! GO BUY ANOTHER PAIR OF SIX-HUNDRED-DOLLAR BOOTS WITH YOUR BIG SALARY!!

KALINA. I DON'T NEED THIS SHIT FROM YOU!! I AM PERSON. I AM NOT TO BE TREATED LIKE THE GARBAGE!!

CASH. YEAH, YEAH, YEAH, GO LIVE IN A DUMPSTER, YOU FUCKING MORON!!

KALINA. I HATE YOU, I HATE YOU, I HATE YOU!!

She throws wine in CASH*'s face and storms up the stairs.*

CASH (*calmer*). Idiot.

Pause. Then, quite audibly, a noise overhead. All look up. We hear something move or roll from one side of the ceiling to the other. All follow with their eyes.

CAROL. Now, *that* I heard.

CLAY (*possessed with fury*). I knew it. I knew it. I knew it. Goddammit, goddammit, goddamm . . .

He races off toward the kitchen. We hear slamming noises. CAROL *hands* CASH *a dish towel as* KAYLA *tugs at her sleeve.*

CAROL (*to* KAYLA). What, sweetheart?

CAROL *bends down and* KAYLA *whispers in her ear.* CLAY *returns with flashlight on his way to the front.*

CLAY. . . . goddammit, goddammit . . .

CAROL (*to* KAYLA). Ohhh, well, of *course* I will. Why didn't you say so?

Taking KAYLA*'s hand, the two of them begin to exit as* KALINA*, in coat and scarf, comes stomping down the stairs, crying loudly. Mascara pours down her cheeks. She storms out of the front door, leaving it wide open.*

CLAY. It's either on the roof or in the crawl space. Did you hear it again?

He grabs a golf club as he exits through the front door.

CASH. So, this paedophile goes to a circumcision . . .

CLAY (*racing back in through the front door*). I'm pretty sure I saw something run to the other side. I don't know what it is but I swear to God it was something!!

He exits out to the back. KAYLA *and* CAROL *are gone.* CASH *and* KELLY *are alone.*

KELLY (*to* CASH). Well, this has certainly been a real pleasure.

CASH. Thanks for having me.

KELLY. And now perhaps you could get the fuck out.

CASH (*to the* BABY, *as he rises to go*). Wow. Hey, Junior. That's some bitter milk you're drinking there.

From outside we hear CLAY *throwing rocks at the roof.*

CLAY. Get outta here!! Get away from my house!! *Yaaah!!*

KELLY. If you hurry maybe you can find yourself some more adolescent Eurotrash beaver.

A crash from upstairs. Breaking glass. A piercing burglar alarm starts to sound. Exterior floodlights turn on. KELLY *remains seated.* CLAY *races in, out of breath.*

CLAY (*shouting to be heard*). I BROKE A WINDOW! I THOUGHT I SAW IT SO I THREW THE CLUB BUT I BROKE THE WINDOW! DO YOU HAVE THE ALARM KEY?!

KELLY (*the same*). I GAVE IT TO YOU!

CLAY (*searching through his keys*). I THOUGHT I GAVE IT TO YOU!!

KELLY. YOU WERE THE LAST ONE TO HAVE IT!

CLAY (*searching his pockets*). AT FIRST I THOUGHT IT MIGHT BE A RACCOON, BUT IT'S MOVING TOO FAST TO BE A RACCOON!

CASH. MAYBE IT'S AN ADOLESCENT EUROTRASH BEAVER!

CLAY (*to* KELLY). I DON'T HAVE IT! WHAT AM I SUPPOSED TO DO?!

KELLY. WELL, CLAY, THE ALARM ISN'T GOING TO SHUT OFF ALL BY ITSELF!

The alarm shuts off all by itself. Lights change. MR HADID *has a question.*

MR HADID. Excuse me?

CLAY (*out of breath*). Yeah?

MR HADID. One more question.

CLAY. Uh-huh?

MR HADID. This neighbourhood?

CLAY. Right?

MR HADID. In a neighbourhood such as this one, what can one expect to pay for property tax?

CLAY *stares.*

CLAY. I . . . in *what*?

MR HADID. That is, with a house of this size and with the school district, upon what basis would the figure be calculated? The property tax?

CLAY (*growing frustrated*). Um . . . yeah. I, uh, sorry. I have to say this. Not to be critical? But I kind of get the feeling that . . . that maybe you're not really listening to what we're trying to *say.*

MR HADID. I am sorry.

CLAY. I mean, the *property ta – who cares*? That's not the point, all right? This isn't about . . . where did we get the table or . . . how much were my . . . I mean, *come on.* Okay? Come on.

MR HADID. I apologise.

CLAY. It's not what *we're about.*

MR HADID. Then, if you wish, you may tell me what you are about.

Pause.

CLAY. Basically we're about the family.

MR HADID. *Your* family.

CLAY. No.

MR HADID. You are not for *my* family.

CLAY. No. I'm only talking about advantages. Giving your child every possible advantage.

MR HADID. Advantage over *my* child.

CLAY. No, Jesus, *come on.* Don't make me talk in clichés. There is an intrinsic value, right, to . . . ? Look. Parents and children –

MR HADID. Your children.

CLAY. No.

MR HADID. You are for your children. And I am for my children.

CLAY. I disagree.

MR HADID. Why would you be for my children? For my family? This makes no sense.

CLAY. Because . . . wait a second . . . you're not looking at who we are.

MR HADID. And this is the reason why you kill people.

Pause.

CLAY. No.

MR HADID. You kill people.

CLAY. No.

MR HADID. Yes. If it serves your family. You would kill them.

CLAY. No.

MR HADID. As I would do for mine.

CLAY. You're looking at it all wrong.

MR HADID. For your family. This is only how it is. And this is the reason why you kill my wife.

CAROL. *Clay?!*

The alarm resumes at full blast. The lights resume. CAROL *returns with* KAYLA *in tow.* KELLY *stands and goes to the alarm box.* CAROL *places* KAYLA *on top of the coffee table. In one hand she holds* KAYLA*'s pull-up, and with the other she lifts* KAYLA*'s skirt to peer underneath.* KELLY *switches off the alarm.*

KELLY (*to* CLAY, *key in hand*). The key was sitting right on top of the box.

CAROL. Clay?

CLAY. Huh?

CAROL. I'm sorry, but . . . has anyone . . . ? I was changing her little thing here and . . . Oh dear. (*Re.* KAYLA.) Has anybody else seen this?

CLAY *looks at* KELLY. KELLY *looks at* CASH. CASH *looks at* CLAY.

CASH. Maybe I oughta go.

Blackout.

End of Act One.

ACT TWO

Later. CLAY, KELLY *and* KAYLA *sit around the table but no one seems to be eating much. Across the room,* KALINA *lies asleep on the sofa, under her coat, boots off. The remainder of a six-pack of beer dangles from her fingertips.* MR HADID *sits away from the table, not far from* CAROL, *who picks up where she left off.*

CAROL. Anyway. So. Genghis Khan and the Mongol Hordes.

MR HADID. Yes?

CAROL. The documentary? The one on PBS? The one I started to tell you about?

MR HADID. Ah yes.

CAROL. So *good.* Oh, I wish you had seen it! Just for the music alone. When they go charging across the steppes with all the horses and the banners fluttering in the wind? And they establish this magnificent empire? Wonderful. But you didn't see it?

MR HADID. I don't think so.

CAROL. And the narrator was that wonderful actor. That really fine actor. The British actor. And they had an interview with him afterwards and he was saying – this was interesting – he said that the secret to fine acting, that *acting* is actually all about *listening.* Isn't that interesting?

MR HADID. Interesting.

CAROL (*laughs*). I mean, maybe *you* should be an actor because you're such a wonderful *listener.*

MR HADID. Thank you.

CAROL. Not like my husband, I don't mind telling you.

MR HADID. I believe you mentioned your husband.

CAROL. Did I?

MR HADID. That he was not a good listener.

CAROL. Is that right? Well, I guess maybe I did. (*Laughs.*) And see? You *remember*, too! You retain things. Not like me. I've gotten terrible. I'm like that woman in that joke. Where the woman goes to see her doctor?

MR HADID. Yes. You have said this.

CAROL. And the doctor says I'm afraid I have some bad news?

MR HADID. I thought you were going to say I have cancer.

CAROL. Oh. Well, now that's the *punchline*.

MR HADID. Yes, you said this.

CLAY. Mom?

CAROL. Oh, poop. I *did*, didn't I?

MR HADID. Yes.

CLAY. Mom?

CAROL. Well, there you go. But no. My husband? No. In one ear and out the other.

CLAY. Mom?

CAROL (*turning back*). Hmm?

CLAY. Can I have the Brussels sprouts, please?

CAROL. Oh, of course. (*Passes them over.*)

CAROL *turns back to the table and the lights shift to Thanksgiving.* CLAY *slowly serves himself, then:*

CLAY. Anyone else? Brussels sprou – ? (*To* KELLY, *who stares at him.*) What?

KELLY. What?

CLAY. What?

KELLY. Nothing. What?

CLAY. What are you staring at?

KELLY. Who?

CLAY. You were staring.

KELLY. You're the one staring at *me*.

CLAY (*to* CAROL). Mom? Brussels sprouts?

CAROL. Kay-kay? I bet *you're* a Brussels sprout girl! All the special girls I know like a nummy Brussels sprout! And you're special, aren't you? Yes, you are. And Brussels sprouts are the nummiest of the nummy! Aren't they, hmm?

KELLY (*under her breath, re.* CLAY). *Staring.* Paranoid.

CLAY *throws down his fork.*

CLAY. Okay. I give up.

KELLY. Go ahead and *eat*, Clay.

CLAY. Well, I'm *trying* to, aren't I? I seem to be the only one.

KELLY. You'll understand if I don't exactly have an *appetite* at the moment.

CLAY. Well, the interesting thing *is* that people actually can't *survive* without eating.

KELLY. No one's stopping you. Shovel it in.

CLAY. Exactly. So if I eat my dinner –

KELLY (*overlapping*). You want a pleasant meal? Let's have a pleasant meal.

CLAY (*continuous*) – somehow that demonstrates my *indifference to my child*? Is that it?

KELLY. Carol, would you pass the cranberries, please?

CAROL (*doing so*). With *pleasure*.

KELLY. Thank you.

Pause.

CAROL (*to* KAYLA). Sweetheart, you know that sometimes grown-ups get sad, too, don't you? *Yes, they do.* And you know, when that happens, you *know* that doesn't mean Mommy and Daddy are sad because of you, does it? It only means that –

KELLY. Please don't talk down to her like that.

CAROL. I didn't.

KELLY. In that baby voice.

CAROL. I . . . well. All right. You're right. It's not my place.

KELLY (*to* KAYLA). Mommy and Daddy are fighting. You understand that.

KAYLA *nods.* KELLY *shrugs.*

CAROL (*to* KAYLA, *loud whisper*). *But they're not fighting because of you.*

KELLY *glares at* CAROL, *then:*

CLAY. Good salad, Mom.

CAROL. Hm? Oh, well, you're very welcome.

CLAY. These nuts are great.

CAROL. Those are *soy nuts*. Aren't those good?

CLAY. Really good.

KELLY (*to* KAYLA). Use your fork, please.

Pause. Clinking.

CLAY. I was thinking. Maybe after dinner. If you want, we could all play a game of –

KELLY. Clay? Let's just eat and get it over with.

CLAY. Well, you know what? We're all going to have to *go on living somehow*, I mean –

KELLY (*overlapping*). A *game*? What, you feel like playing a *board game*?

CLAY (*continuous*). – as far as I can tell . . . Wait. Let me check. Yes. The earth is *still revolving*.

CAROL. Kay-kay? Are you done with your dinner now? Maybe you and I could watch a cartoon!

KELLY. A *game*. Yeah, let's all play *Yahtzee*.

CLAY. Fine. Okay, fine. I can't win. I can't. Why don't I just *move out*?

KELLY. Carol? Are you finished?

CLAY. Why don't I just go upstairs and *hang* myself?

CAROL (*to* KELLY). Not quite.

CLAY. Never mind that I'm the only person who seems to be capable of taking some *action*.

KELLY. But Clay

CLAY. While everyone else stands around with their thumb up their ass.

KELLY. But think for a moment.

CLAY. I don't need to think –

KELLY. What good does it do to take an action when –

CLAY (*continuous, overlapping*). What I *need* is to protect the health of my child!

KELLY (*continuous*). – when you're not in possession of all the *facts*? And please stop using Kayla to justify yourself.

CLAY. Okay. Clearly I'm worthless. Clearly I'm horrible.

CAROL. Oh, Clay, stop it.

CLAY. I'll get a rope or maybe a belt. And I'll just hang myself.

CAROL. You've been very judgemental. All evening.

CLAY. Right. Right. I see.

CAROL. And it's very *oppressive* to be judged.

KELLY. It would be one thing if you had all the facts. But you just get on the phone and blindly take the law into your own hands.

CLAY (*to* KELLY). Do you want me to call back? I'll call them back right now, if you want.

KELLY. It's too late *now*.

  KALINA *begins muttering in her sleep.*

KALINA (*anguished*). *Nemojte! Molimvas, nemojte! Necu da udjem, necu!* [NEH-moy-tay! MOH-leem-vas, NEH-moy-tay! NEH-choo dah OOD-jem, NEH-choo!]

  All turn for a moment, then go on.

CLAY. So what do you want me to do? You tell me.

KELLY. I want you to get all the *facts*.

CAROL. I'm not surprised Cash stays away.

CLAY (*to* CAROL). Oh-ho-ho-ho-*ho*. Don't *even*. I will *kill*. I will reach across this table and actively *kill*.

CAROL. Well, I'm *sorry*. But his holiday was ruined.

CLAY (*seething*). Ohhh, my *God*. Mother of *God*.

KELLY. There are a *number* of possible explanations.

CLAY. Mom? (*To* KELLY.) Excuse me. (*To* CAROL.) Mom? I happen to discover that – (*Lowers voice.*) – my daughter's health has been seriously compromised? And you say to me I ruined that prick's holiday?!

CAROL. Cash didn't do anything to you.

CLAY. Oh, right. Oh, *never*. You know what? Just say to me *I prefer Cash in all things. I always have and I always will prefer Cash to you.*

KELLY (*rising*). Carol? If you'll excuse me from the *festival of regurgitation*?

CLAY. Cash, who apparently can't even fulfil the basic requirement of the human *species. Reproduce!*

CAROL (*to* KELLY, *who has begun to clear*). I didn't use my spoon.

KELLY (*to* CAROL). It's all going in the dishwasher.

CLAY. And if you can't accomplish *that*, well, I'm sorry, but I'd have to say you're *disqualified* from the species! Case closed.

CAROL. Well, see? Now you're judging *Cash*.

CLAY (*pointing to* KAYLA). Look at that. Look at that child. *That* is the future, Mom. *We* live on. *We* succeed. Cash? No. Cash dies and his genes die with him! And guess what? Those are *your genes too*!

CAROL. You sound completely ridiculous.

CLAY. Ruined his *holiday*. Oh, what a *shame*. What a goddam *shame*.

The phone begins to ring. CLAY *rises.*

CAROL. Cash is not the enemy.

CLAY. Let's go kill the fatted calf for *Cash's holiday*.

KELLY (*to* KAYLA). Sweetie? Are you done?

KELLY *helps* KAYLA *down*.

CAROL. You have a *great* many blessings. There's no reason to take things out on –

CLAY (*stopping on his way to the phone*). Sorry? What? What's that supposed to mean?

CAROL. Nothing.

CLAY. No, no, no. Don't try to back out of it.

CAROL. I meant nothing.

CLAY. I heard the inflection. 'A *great* many.' That's how you said it.

CAROL. Well, you do.

CLAY. And raising your eyebrows like that. Like with some kind of *disapproval*?

CAROL. I don't disapprove.

CLAY. Oh really?

CAROL. I only say that with such a *great* number of blessings –

CLAY. The eyebrows! You did it again.

CAROL. With such *great* blessings –

CLAY. Right there! You keep doing it! Just admit what you're doing.

CAROL. – one oughtn't have to be judgemental.

The phone is still ringing.

CLAY. Oh-oh. So you're calling us *rich*.

KELLY (*re. phone*). Are you going to get that?

CLAY (*to* CAROL). You people are obsessed with our money. Try to grasp this concept: We are – (*Quietly.*) – *barely fucking scraping by.* We are *so* not *rich*.

KELLY. Clay?

CLAY. Do you have any idea of the financing on a place like this?

CAROL. Well, what does that tell you?

CLAY. This isn't *liquid*. Jesus, it's an investment!

CAROL. Well, there are people in the world –

CLAY. That doesn't make us *rich*.

CAROL. Some people would *like* to be called rich.

CLAY. If it *applied*. And, in this case, it *doesn't*.

KELLY. CLAY!

CLAY (*finally answering*). Hello?

We hear a car arriving.

CAROL. I think you have some sort of *guilt complex*.

CLAY (*phone*). Yeah. No. No, she's here now. No, she's on the sofa.

CAROL. I wish someone would call *me* rich.

CLAY (*phone*). No, *asleep* on the sofa. About half an hour ago. No, she couldn't because you have her credit cards. Well, where are you?

KELLY (*to* CAROL *as she exits to kitchen*). I'm going to cover this with foil.

CAROL. Just use that plastic wrap.

CLAY (*phone*). No, I won't. Because she's asleep. Well, maybe that's not our problem, okay?

The front door opens and CASH *walks in, cellphone to his ear – he has been talking to* CLAY.

CAROL (*to* KAYLA). Do you want to go help Mommy?

CLAY (*phone, not yet noticing* CASH). Maybe *you* have to *work that out for yourself*. Does that ring a bell? Huh? Where do you suppose you might have heard that particular turn of phrase before? Hmm? That stir up any memories for you?

CASH. Hey, Mom.

CLAY *turns. They both hang up.*

CAROL. Is that . . . ? Oh, *poop*. And we just *finished*! Poop, poop, *poop*!

CASH (*approaching* KALINA). Doesn't matter.

CAROL. Sit, sit. Let me fix you a plate.

CLAY. Hang on. No. Mom?

CAROL. Just a little plate.

CLAY. Right, but we're not in the eating stage now, are we? Now we're in the *cleaning-up* stage.

CAROL. But Cash didn't get any food.

CLAY. Well, unfortunately now the food is being *wrapped up*.

CAROL (*to* CASH). How about a little stuffing?

CLAY. And that applies to the stuffing.

CASH. Hey, Mom? I'm not hungry.

CAROL. But you were out there driving around. You need something warm.

CASH. We're not gonna stay.

CAROL. Well, I'm making you a plate.

CLAY (*taking a seat*). Guess I was wrong. Guess we're still eating, then.

CAROL. Clay, stop it.

CLAY (*sitting*). Right. Okay, back to the table! Everybody sit down!

KELLY *re-enters*.

KELLY (*flat*). Oh, look who's back.

CASH (*re.* KALINA). I'm just gonna grab her and go.

KELLY. Stay. You and Clay play a board game.

CLAY. Is no one else sitting? *I'm* sitting.

KELLY. A quick round of Stratego.

CAROL (*dishing out a plate*). What about this casserole? How about some of that?

CASH. Mom? Seriously. I'm not hungry, okay?

CAROL. Well, at least some coffee.

CLAY. We don't have coffee.

CAROL. Oh, there's *plenty* of coffee.

CLAY. Not *made* there's not.

CAROL. Well, it's easy enough to make *coffee*.

CLAY. Well, I didn't want to make coffee. (*To* KELLY.) Did you?

KELLY. Did I what?

CLAY. Want to make coffee?

KELLY. When? At what point?

CLAY. I mean *do* you?

KELLY. Strange way to ask.

CAROL. I mean, I personally don't want coffee, but maybe Cash . . . ?

CASH. You know what? We're not gonna stay.

CLAY. No, stay. Gonna have *coffee*.

CASH. No coffee for me.

CAROL (*to* CLAY). Or maybe – (*Re.* KALINA.) – she'd like coffee, because of . . . ? (*Mimes drinking.*)

CASH. Mom? Never mind. They have a whole elaborate . . . process . . . so.

CLAY (*as though considering this*). 'Elaborate'? Our coffee?

CASH. With the grinding and so forth.

CLAY. And that strikes you as *elaborate*.

CAROL (*raising her hand*). Let's have a show of hands. Because I *don't* want coffee.

CASH. I dunno, Clay. However you guys make it.

CLAY. Wasn't aware you had all these thoughts about our *coffee*.

CASH. It's extraordinary coffee. It's superior coffee.

KELLY (*putting it to rest*). So actually, *no one* wants coffee. Is that right?

CLAY. 'Elaborate.' Huh. Fascinating.

KALINA begins muttering again in her agitated way.

KALINA (*asleep*). *Stiscem me! Oww! Boli me ruka! Pustite me! Ocu kuci. Ne! Ne!* [STEESH-chem meh! Oww! BOH-lee meh ROO-kah! POOS-tee-tay meh! OH-choo KOO-chee. NEH! NEH!]

Pause. All stare. CASH jiggles KALINA's foot.

CASH (*to KALINA*). Hey.

CAROL. Oh, let her be. She looks so . . . *oh, oh look.* Is she *sucking her thumb*? Isn't that *adorable*? She looks like she could be *five years old.*

KELLY (*to CASH*). When does puberty usually hit?

CASH (*to KALINA*). C'mon.

CAROL. Cash, *don't.*

KALINA (*coming round*). Why? What? What is happening?

CASH. Time to go.

KALINA (*bleary, but registering, and resenting CASH*). Don't do that to me. Stop it. (*She turns to CAROL instead.*) What? What did I do? What time is it now?

CAROL. About nine-thirty.

KALINA. Nooo, no. Now you are silly. Is *dark* outside.

CLAY. Nine-thirty at *night.*

KALINA. No. I was sleeping.

CAROL. You just took a little *nap.*

KALINA. No. I was so *sleepy.* And also not feeling so good.

KELLY. Yeah, malt liquor'll do that to you.

CASH. Let's get outta here.

KALINA (*angry whisper*). Please do not be touching me.
(*Changing the subject.*) Ohhhh! *Heyyy!* Look! It is Kayla!
It is Kayleetchka!! Hey, you come and sit with me now,
yes? Huh? Because now we are going to be like sisters!
I will be the big sister!!

KAYLA *does so.*

KELLY. Sweetie, time for bed.

KALINA (*to* KAYLA). Hey, and look! Look, there is our
mommy!! Our mommy, the beauteous Kelly who is so
perfect in all things and is also being the simultaneous *sex
goddess*, huh? Are we so lucky, huh? To have the mommy
who is the perfect *sex goddess*?

KELLY. Kayla?

KALINA. Oh, Kelly, you know? Is all I ever wanted, is to be
part of family like this!

CAROL. I assumed you *had* family.

KALINA. No, Carol. Is sad for me.

KELLY. We assumed they were circus people.

KALINA (*laughs*). Ohhh, noo! Kelly is crazy. (*To* KAYLA.)
Our mommy is crazy to joke with me. (*To* KELLY.) You
mean like the gypsies?! (*Laughs.*) Believe me, Kelly. I will
tell you about the gypsies. (*Puts hand to head.*) Ow. I maybe
am needing the coffee. There is coffee?

CAROL (*whispering to* CASH *as she goes*). Just a *little plate,*
is all.

CAROL *exits to kitchen.*

KELLY (*taking* KAYLA *by the hand and leading her upstairs*).
Come on. Time for bed.

KALINA (*to* KAYLA *as they go*). Kayla Kayleetchka! You know this, yes? That I cannot have the children? Due to the scar tissue the doctor put on my uterus? But if is not for the scar tissue on my uterus I would have *twenty* Kaylas just like *you*!

The BABY *starts to cry upstairs.* KELLY *lifts* KAYLA *and carries her up.*

CASH (*to* KALINA, *as* KELLY *and* KAYLA *exit*). Hey.

KALINA. Hey? Hey, to *me*, you say? No. Not hey. Hey, *you*. *You*, hey. And here is other funny thing. Funny thing is how I am talking to *them* and not to *you*.

CASH (*sighing*). I'm sorry if I raised my voi –

KALINA. Almost as funny as how I am a nitwit, but still have to take orders from you? That is funny. (*To* CLAY.) And this also is something funny which you can tell him from me. How I am not just a little . . . uhh . . . machine for to give him the blow jobs, you know? He can buy for himself machine if he wants only to have the blow jobs on the regular base. (*Thinks.*) Regular *base*?

CLAY. Basis.

KALINA. Regular *basis*. For this, he can save money, get himself *machine*.

CASH. Where would I find such a machine?

KALINA. And for what am I to be this machine? So that I can have place to live? Ha. I think *fuck this*. I can go to hotel, maybe. And you will tell him this from me.

CASH. We had *assumed* you'd been hit by a truck.

KALINA (*shrugs*). Would make you happy, maybe.

CASH. Little did we know. You just popped over to the mini-mart.

KALINA. What do you care? I am just a nitwit.

CASH. As I'm driving round out there for an hour and a half.

KALINA. So go away.

CASH. You do *know* they don't want you here? You do *know* this?

KALINA. How do you know?

CASH. Oh, I have a feeling.

KALINA. So you are expert now?

CASH. I just get a feeling.

KALINA. You don't even talk to them. I am talking to them. Because now we are friends, you know? (*To* CLAY.) Is true, yes? How now we are friends?

CLAY. Sure.

KALINA (*as a secret*). Is because he is *jealous*. Is true, you know? Of you and Kelly. Even with all the problems. Still he is jealous.

CLAY. The problems.

KALINA. The problems with the marriage. Is no big deal.

CLAY (*to* CASH, *calmly*). Uh-huh. *We* have problems. I see.

KALINA. Oooch. My stomach is also not so good.

CLAY (*to* CASH). I mean, *problems*? Okay, yeah. Problems *arise*. But you know what? The interesting thing about problems? You *work them out*. That's what adults *do*.

KALINA. I tell you, he is not happy person.

CLAY (*to* KALINA). But, of course, he wouldn't *know* that. Because *my* experience? My experience is, if you go to *Cash* with your problems? Cash's response is: *you guys work it out on your own*.

KALINA. *He* is the one who is like the gypsy, your brother.

CLAY (*to* CASH). I mean, seriously. Who's really the one with the *problems*?

KALINA. Is true. Because the gypsies, you see, they will always cheat you and steal from you and lie to you and they act like, *hey, so what? Is cool. Is no big deal!*

CLAY. Exactly.

KALINA. And I tell you something. If I was president of *my* country. This is true. If *I* was the president, I would get all of the gypsies, and take them to some place, and get rid of them.

She breezily draws a finger across her throat and makes a slashing sound.

All of them. Is nothing else to do. Is nothing but to get rid of them. Is exactly the way it was with the Jews.

CAROL *enters with a plate of food.*

CAROL (*quietly, to* CASH). Now, I didn't give you any green beans because I know how you feel about green beans.

KELLY (*from upstairs*). Oh my God. Oh God. *Clay?*

CASH (*to* KALINA). Let's go.

KALINA. I am not going with you.

KAYLA, *in her pyjamas enters from above. She carries a videotape.*

CAROL (*to* KAYLA). Well, look who's *here*. Are you all ready for sleepy-sleep?

KELLY *appears behind* KAYLA, *holding an avocado between tissues.*

KELLY (*quietly intense*). It was in her *room*, Clay. That animal was in her *room*. Oh God, *look at this.*

CAROL (*to* KAYLA). Look at this lonely empty lap. Is that your cartoon? Hmm?

KELLY (*quietly, so as not to alarm* KAYLA). Wedged behind her My Little Pony House. (*Nauseous.*) Ohhh God. Teeth marks. I'm gonna be sick.

CASH (*calling out to the room*). Goodnight. I'm leaving.

KALINA (*to* CASH). Give me the credit cards.

CASH (*extracting his wallet*). Why, certainly. Would that be the Mastercard you haven't paid for two years?

KELLY. How could it *carry* an *avocado*?

CASH. Or maybe you'd prefer the Amex with the balance of seventeen thousand dollars?

CLAY (*wheeling on* CASH). Hey, would you stop hassling her?

CASH (*laughs*). What??

CLAY. She's free to do what –

CASH. *Hassling* her?

CLAY. Just let her –

CASH. I shouldn't *hassle* her?

CLAY. Just leave her alone.

CASH. Whatever you say, *Billy Jack*.

KELLY (*to* CLAY). Just let them go.

CASH (*to* KALINA). I could physically overpower you. I can *put* you in the car. Is that what you want?

CAROL (*to* KAYLA, *who now sits in her lap*). Kay-kay, some people think that just because they're bigger and stronger they get to always have their way in the world. But we know that's not true.

CASH. Hey, Kayla? Do you know the phrase *sanitised for your protection*?

CLAY (*to* KALINA). You can sleep on the sofa.

KELLY. Wait, wait, wait, wait, wait.

CLAY. No. Let him go. He didn't want to be here in the first place. He has no interest in this family.

CASH. Clay, I'm *sorry*. I'm *sorry* your kid is sick, okay? I'm *sorry*.

KALINA. Oh, Kayleetchka? You are not feeling so good?

KELLY (*to* CASH). Don't, okay? Not in front of –

CASH. We all *know*. Why do we have to act like . . . ?

CAROL (*to* KALINA). She has a little infection. (*To* KAYLA.) Don't you, Miss Scratchy-Pants?

CASH. We're all sorry, Clay. All right? But the bullshit can get rather *exhausting*.

CLAY. So *our* life is *bullshit*.

CASH. Oh Jesus.

CAROL (*to* KAYLA, *underneath*). We have nothing to be ashamed of. We're *innocent*.

KALINA (*standing unsteadily*). Is bathroom this way?

CLAY (*to* CASH). So you are the great repository of the *truth*.

KELLY. Just *don't*. Just ask the two of them to *leave*.

CLAY. No, no, no. Let's hear the great *truth* that Cash has brought for us.

CAROL (*to* KAYLA). You don't want to watch with me?

CLAY. Let us in on the *big picture*. O great guardian of the wisdom.

CASH (*to* KELLY). What do *you* want me to say? Do *you* have a suggestion?

KALINA. Kelly, do you have some of the Maalox?

CASH (*to* KELLY). Do you really want to have this conversation?

KELLY (*to* CASH). *Shut up!*

CAROL (*to* KAYLA). Who's the specialest person for watching cartoons? Hm? You show me who!

CLAY. Who really has the problems, huh? Slandering us behind our backs.

KALINA (*exiting*). Excuse me, everbody, for my sickness!

CASH. Well, Clay. I don't know what you're going to do to me since *Daddy's* dead. Since you can't go *tattle* on me to someone who'll beat my ass with a *belt* for you. That's a real *quandary*, isn't it? You little sissy-ass *tattle-tale*.

CLAY. Lemme tell you something. *Golf is a very difficult and challenging game.* I'd like to see you *try* it.

KELLY (*overlapping after 'game'*). Clay. End it. Now.

CASH (*overlapping, falsetto, after 'to see'*). Daddy! Cash took my Hot Wheels! Punish Cash, Daddy!

CAROL. I *told* your father if he insisted on calling two boys Cassius and Clay that they were bound to fight.

KAYLA *approaches* CASH. *She points at him.*

CASH (*to* KAYLA). Hey. How you doin'?

KELLY. Kayla? *No.*

CAROL. Ohhh, I don't think *he* wants to watch.

KELLY. Come here, sweetie.

CAROL. I'm a better person for watching cartoons.

CASH (*to* KAYLA). Hey. Look. Wanna see something?

CAROL (*to* KAYLA). *I* like cartoons.

KELLY. Sweetie? Kayla?

CASH. Lemme show you something. Look at this.

CASH *makes his face into a pig-face.* KAYLA *starts to laugh.*

CAROL. Do you want to put in the tape? Let's do that.

CASH (*pig voice*). I am Uncle Pig Face. Do you want to kiss my pig face?

KELLY. Kayla? (*To* CASH.) Leave her alone.

KAYLA *is still laughing.*

CASH (*pig voice*). Greetings, little girl! Come and kiss my pig face! Hahahaha!!

KELLY (*to* CASH). Okay, *out.* I want you out.

CLAY. Kayla, go with Grandma.

KELLY. Now. Go. I'm sorry. I've had it. You can both leave now. You and your underage –

CASH. We're just goofing around.

KELLY. No, no, no. Waltzing into my home. Waltzing in and out of my *life*? I mean, *who do you think you are*? I've had it, okay?

CASH. *Waltzing?*

KELLY. Waltzing in like you got the keys to the place? How *dare* you.

CASH. Thought I was doing the *foxtrot.*

KELLY. I've simply . . . oh God, I fucking HAAATE YOU! I would so gladly slice off your balls and cram them up your . . . (*Strangled shriek.*) HAAATE YOU!!

A miserable silence. Finally:

CAROL (*to* KAYLA, *taking her by the hand*). I'm going to put on *my* jammies. Do you think you can help me do that? Hmm?

CAROL *and* KAYLA *exit up the stairs. The silence returns. Then, from off, we hear* KALINA *retching.* CASH *stands.*

CASH. I . . . uhh . . . I'm gonna . . . (*Indicates bathroom.*) I'll see what's . . . Yeah.

CASH *goes.* KELLY *begins to cry.*

CLAY. Shhh. C'mon. I know.

KELLY. No, you don't.

CLAY. I can take care of it.

KELLY. No, you can't.

CLAY. I'll take her to the right people. I swear.

KELLY. I . . . but . . . you don't –

CLAY. Listen to me. I can handle it.

KELLY. I just . . . why did you have to . . . I mean . . . ?

CLAY. What?

KELLY. Oh God, Clay. I'm just really *sad* right now. Okay?
I'm *sad*.

He kneels close to her as she cries.

CLAY. Hey. Hey. Shhh. Come on. I know. It's all scary. This is
scary stuff and I'm scared, too. But I told them everything we
know. And possibly it's nothing. But if not. If it's something
bad. Something some person did. Some sick sort of . . .

She cries more, he embraces her.

Hey. Ohhh, sweetie. Look at you. Look at your face. You're
so beautiful. Don't you know how amazing you are? You're
in the *dictionary* under 'amazing'. Hey. We're still us.
We're still the same two crazy . . . *people*. Hey, remember
when I had that *beard*? Remember that? Why did I shave
that off? I gotta grow another bea –

KELLY (*recoiling*). Clay. Your *breath*.

CLAY. Whoops.

Pause. He backs off.

KELLY. And I hated that beard.

CLAY. Well.

KELLY. It was like kissing a vagina.

Pause.

CLAY. Tell you what, *Groucho*. As soon as everyone leaves.
Mom goes to sleep. *I* am going to load up the *magic pipe*.

KELLY. I don't want to get *stoned*, Clay. I have a *career*.
I don't want to spend *my* life getting *stoned* like some kind
of deadbeat *loser*.

CLAY. I didn't mean –

KELLY. 'The same two crazy peo – ' What does that *mean*?
Why do you have to use these *clichés*, these stultifying little
predigested . . . God . . . why do you have to –

CLAY (*overlapping*). Okay.

KELLY (*continuing*). – incessantly *do* that?

CLAY. Okay. O . . . *kay*. Here's what I'm gonna do.

KELLY. I don't think I love you any more.

Pause.

I don't think I've loved you for about four years.

CLAY. Huh?

KELLY (*sobbing again*). Oh God. Oh God.

CLAY. Well, here's what *I* think. I *thought* that we'd worked
through all this. That's what *I* thought.

KELLY. Apparently not.

CLAY. Apparently not. Apparently we didn't.

We hear CAROL from upstairs.

CAROL (*to* KAYLA). Grammy's in her jammies. Are we
going to brush our teeth now?

CLAY. So *apparently* when we said to the doctor, said that all
of the problems seem to be resolved, water under the
bridge, what was I thinking, of course I love my husband,
apparently when we were sitting in that office saying all
that, *apparently* one of us wasn't exactly telling the truth, is
that right?

KELLY (*pauses, then*). I didn't say –

CLAY. Well, you know, the thing is, if you *pause* before you answer? When I ask these questions? Then I think it means you're about to lie to me. So: were you telling the truth?

Pause.

Pause . . .

KELLY. Don't tell me how I'm supposed to answer.

CLAY. Well, what would you expect me to think? Wouldn't that be the natural assumption? In the space of the pause?

KELLY. No.

CLAY. That would be *my* assumption.

KELLY. Well, that's *you*.

CLAY. If *I* heard someone pause in that way.

KELLY. Well, you're not me.

CLAY. So were you?

Pause. CLAY *nods.*

Pause . . .

KELLY. I'm *upset,* Clay! Can't you see how I *feel*?

CASH *has entered, holding a bathmat.*

CASH. Whoops.

CLAY. No, no. Stay. Please. This is good.

KELLY. Please don't.

CASH (*not sure whether to stay or go*). Sorry.

CLAY. This is good. Now he can see what he missed.

KELLY. Not with him here.

CLAY. But we're *family*, right? This is my family. And when I call my family, four years or *whatever* ago, and I say help me, can you help me out, I think my wife may be in love with someone else and my family member says to me, says in this tone of voice, says, you guys work it out on your own, like that, see, then he never gets to see what it was really *like*. What it's like to pay some doctor a hundred and fifty bucks a week just so that *one* of us can make up stories about how, *now*, everything is just *fine*.

KELLY. *You* didn't pay.

CLAY (*to* CASH). True. I didn't pay. *She* paid so that *she* could make up stories.

KELLY. Right, because I'm such a *liar.*

CLAY. No. Hey. If you want to throw away your money making up little *stories.*

KELLY (*as much for* CASH*'s benefit as* CLAY*'s*). I'm not the one with the giant closet full of *porn*. All right? I'm sick of it. I throw that shit out and two weeks later there's twice as much. I'm fucking *sick* of it. Sixteen-year-old girls in high heels with *come* dripping off their chins. It's fucking *disgusting*. I want it out of my house. It *disgusts* me.

KALINA (*from the bathroom*). Cash?

CASH (*re. the bathmat*). I'm just gonna toss this.

KELLY. But somehow it's *me* that can't be believed.

CLAY. So . . .

KELLY. Is *that* what your notion of family is all about? Huh? If two people love each other, wouldn't you at *least* expect one of them to believe what the other one says?

CLAY (*smug, to* CASH). But see, she just got through telling me that she *doesn't* love me any more.

KELLY *sighs, exhausted.*

KELLY. I still love you.

CLAY. That was persuasive.

KELLY. Oh God, would you STOP IT?!

KALINA *stumbles in, dishevelled.*

KALINA (*like an orphaned child*). Cash, I want to go home.

CASH. Me too.

KALINA (*holding him for support*). I had too many beers.

CASH. I know.

KALINA (*climbing into his arms*). And I think I ruin their bathmat.

CASH. They'll buy a new bathmat.

KELLY (*quietly, to* CLAY). Can't you at least put your arms around me?

CLAY. I don't think I will at the moment.

Now CAROL *is entering from above.*

CAROL (*calling out to an unseen* KAYLA). I'm putting the cartoon in now! But someone I know has to help me push the buttons!

CASH. Let's put your boots on.

KALINA. Those boots, they give me such *blister.*

CASH. I know.

KALINA. For boots this expensive? Is total rip-off.

CASH. We'll get you some new boots.

CAROL (*calling upstairs*). Who's going to help me watch the cartoon?!

KALINA (*petulantly*). Is hard word, you know?

CASH. What word?

KALINA. Per–skeptive.

CASH. I know.

KELLY (*quietly*). Please, Clay. What do you possibly want me to say?

CLAY (*calmly*). Well, I have a suggestion. I don't know, I'll just toss this out. *Possibly* you could say this: see, you *might* say, I'm the person who made Clay kill his cat. How would that feel? So that I could have a couple of babies. Does that work for you? I made him kill his cat so that I could have some babies, and now I'm thinking maybe I'd like to go off and fuck someone else. Try that if you want. Clay had a cat named Chester. *I* forced him to kill it. And now I think I want to . . .

But KELLY *has already exited.*

CAROL (*standing by the TV*). Clay? I . . . I . . . I'm not sure I know how to work this.

Everyone turns. Instead of cartoons, the TV screen is filled with graphic images from a porn video. A man and woman are getting it on. Much grunting and thrusting. No one knows what to do. KALINA *busts out laughing.*

I mean, it's not that I disapprove.

CASH *turns to* MR HADID. *The TV fades out. The afternoon light returns, as does the snow. The others exit.*

CASH. So okay. So listen to this. So the other day this woman comes in my office. Says, to me, I think I want to get a nose job.

MR HADID. I'm sorry. Is this a joke?

CASH. No. True story.

MR HADID. It takes the form of a joke.

CASH (*thinks*). Yeah, I guess it does. So she says, Doc, I want to get a nose job. The problem is – and get this, she says to me – the problem is, I don't believe in plastic surgery. I say, wait a second. I'm sorry, what? She says, not *believe like it doesn't exist*, it's that my belief system tells me not to agree with it. So I say, okay, which belief system is this? She says it's my personal belief. I think it's wrong. I don't think our lives should be determined by something so random as

biology. I think that people should stop being hung up on
the superficial. I have a wonderful personality. I'm a good
friend. I'm funny. I'm lively. And still I don't have a boyfriend
and I don't get the jobs I want. I'm at this enormous
disadvantage all because I've got this nose. She says the
world should not be that way. And that is what I believe.
I believe it. And she says, so what can you say to me to put
my mind at ease about the whole procedure? (*He thinks.*)
Now, I'm trying to wrap my head around this. I'm trying to
get this. I really am. I'm the doctor. Obviously I can't just
act like . . . So I look at her. I put on a serious expression.
And I say, well, let me ask you this: Which do you think
came first, your *beliefs*, or your nose? Because maybe, and I
could be wrong, correct me if I am, but *maybe* if you hadn't
been born with this giant . . . *with* this nose, you wouldn't
have developed these beliefs. She says, yes, but my beliefs
go deeper. My beliefs are who I really *am*. And I say, yes,
right, understood, but see, the problem is, I can't *see* your
beliefs. Whereas your *nose*, to put it mildly, is readily
apparent. And she says, you're acting like my beliefs aren't
serious. And I say, as gently as I can, I say, well, perhaps
not serious *enough* since you're already here for the nose
job. And she says, I don't care for your attitude and I say
okay. So she storms out. Goes to a friend of mine. He fixed
her nose last week. Chin implant, too. My point is . . . well,
you see what my point is

MR HADID. I see what your point is.

Pause.

CASH. So let me ask you something. You don't see the, uh,
irony in all this?

MR HADID. In this situation?

CASH. You drive a cab, right? Is that right?

MR HADID. Yes.

CASH. It's a job.

MR HADID. It is all right.

CASH. Make a decent living.

MR HADID. I make a living.

CASH. Decent.

MR HADID. I do not know what you think is decent.

CASH. You're not starving.

MR HADID. No.

CASH. Maybe not *rolling in dough*.

MR HADID. No.

CASH. But you're not starving.

MR HADID. I am not starving.

CASH. But you got to pay the bills, right?

MR HADID. Yes.

CASH. You're not a *hermit*. You're not some *saint*.

MR HADID. No.

CASH. Some saintly . . . You're not *Gandhi*. You live in the world.

MR HADID. I am not Gandhi.

CASH. Got your cab. Got your home. You got a kid, right? A boy, right?

MR HADID. I have a son, yes.

CASH. Just saying. People aren't that complicated.

MR HADID. I think you are probably right.

CASH. It's like actors, right? What actors say: what's my motivation?

MR HADID. *My* motivation?

CASH. You know. What people want? Why you're here?

MR HADID. You invited me here.

CASH. Not *here* here. I mean in a broader sense. All you want is some of what we have. Right? That's all. Certain advantages. I don't blame you. Who wouldn't? Otherwise why would you have come here in the first place? But don't you see the rather comic dimension of it all? You don't? Look, you want to be more like us . . . (*Laughs.*) But we're a bunch of assholes.

The afternoon light returns from the beginning of the play. Snow begins to fall again. KELLY enters with a glass.

KELLY (*to* MR HADID). This might be the last of the apple juice.

MR HADID. Thank you very much.

KELLY. It's not very cold.

MR HADID. It will be fine.

    CAROL *follows with a plate of cookies.*

CAROL (*to* MR HADID). I know you said you didn't want these. But just in case.

MR HADID. Thank you.

    CAROL *sits next to* CASH.

CAROL (*to* KELLY). I mean, the funny thing is, I vaguely remembered that you and Clay had some problems. Way back when. I vaguely did. But, you know, I had assumed that the problems had . . . well, sort of *resolved* themselves.

    CAROL *looks at* CASH *and* KELLY. *They both shake their heads.* KALINA *enters and joins them.*

    (*Turning to* MR HADID.) What about *Charlie Rose*? Do you ever watch that programme?

MR HADID. I am aware of the programme.

CAROL. Oh, isn't he good? He had that actor on the other night. The British actor? (*To* CASH.) Do you know the one I mean?

CASH *shrugs.*

I wish that I could have a British accent. Don't you? It just sounds so intelligent. (*She tries it out.*) I say. Care for a spot of tea? (*She laughs.*) Cheerio! (*Sighs.*) Anyway. He said, this actor said, that the secret to acting, aside from listening, the secret is that you should like your character. Have you heard that?

MR HADID. I have not heard that.

CLAY *enters and joins them, dressed as before.*

CAROL. And you know, I am just *addicted* to *Antiques Roadshow.*

And now for the first time they are all gathered around MR HADID. *They stare uncomfortably.*

CLAY. Anyway.

KELLY. Anyway.

CAROL. So . . .

CASH. But enough about *me*.

CAROL (*laughs, embarrassed*). Yes, look how we just keep *going on.*

CLAY (*explaining to* MR HADID, *re.* CASH). He's . . . uhh, that's a joke that people . . . If they've been talking all about themselves at length, you know, they say, but enough about *me,* what do *you* think about me? Kind of a joke.

KALINA (*re.* CASH). But we were not talking about him.

CLAY. No, I know, but . . . but . . .

KELLY. But it's emblematic, right? Of the way we're perceived?

CAROL. Oh, *I* get it.

KELLY. As a nation that for some reason just can't seem to keep its big *trap* shut.

CAROL. What do *you* think about . . . That *is* funny.

KELLY. You know. Hopelessly in love with the sound of our own voices.

CLAY. Not all of us. Not *all*.

KELLY. I'm saying that's the *perception*.

CAROL. Oh, I disagree.

CLAY. Then it's a *misperception*.

CAROL. I think other people *envy* us.

KELLY. But how would we know if they do?

CAROL. They do. We have a constitutional democracy.

CLAY. Not for long.

KELLY. No, we soundproof ourselves inside this self-satisfied *echo chamber*, while at the same time broadcasting to the world this empty Starbucks materialism posing as some kind of *dialogue*?

CLAY. But we're not all like that.

KALINA. Why do people make fun of Starbucks? I'm sorry. Is good coffee.

KELLY. And inevitably people are starting to wonder when exactly we intend to *shut up*. But we *don't* intend to shut up. Because we're basically not all that interested in what anyone else has to say.

MR HADID. Excuse me?

CLAY (*to* KELLY). I refuse to accept that.

CAROL. We're *very* interested. That's just not true.

MR HADID. Excuse me?

Pause. All turn to MR HADID.

Forgive me. But you did not finish the story.

KELLY. Uhhh . . . no?

CLAY. Pretty much. Uhh . . . ?

MR HADID. No no no. You have left something out.

CLAY. Uhhh . . . (*To* CAROL.) Did we?

CAROL. No. Not that *I* can think of.

KALINA. Oh yes! The animal! Is true! We are never to find out what kind of weasel it is that has been eating of the avocados!

CAROL. But other than that . . .

KELLY. I don't think so.

CLAY. I don't think we did.

MR HADID. Oh, yes. Yes, you did. Yes, the most important part. The central part.

CLAY. Well, let me think.

MR HADID. The part in which you call the police.

Pause.

CLAY. Oh.

KELLY. Well, *technically* –

CLAY. That wasn't us.

KELLY. That was just the *system*.

CLAY. Not saying *blame the system* –

MR HADID. Some person in this house called the police.

CLAY (*a technicality*). Technically, no.

KELLY. Technically, not *us*.

MR HADID. Oh, yes. I know that this is what happened.

CAROL. But that was much earlier.

CLAY. And not in the way you're thinking.

KELLY. Not like that.

CAROL. That was before the meal.

CLAY. But it wasn't like that.

KELLY. Not at all.

MR HADID. Nevertheless. I would like to hear that part.
    If you would not mind going back. As a favour to me. That
    is the part which I would now like to hear.

*All exchange glances and confused gestures for a few moments.
Then the lights abruptly change. The piercing siren returns.
They stand and resume positions from the end of the first act.
CLAY holds the flashlight. CASH holds his wine-stained shirt.
KELLY is at the alarm box on the wall. KAYLA stands on
the table with her Huggie around her knees. CAROL peers
under KAYLA's skirt. KALINA is gone. The dinner table is
magically reset, complete with burning candles. KELLY turns
the alarm off.*

KELLY (*exactly as before*). The key was sitting right on top of
    the box.

CAROL. Clay?

CLAY. Huh?

CAROL. Has anybody else seen this?

    *CLAY looks at KELLY. KELLY looks at CASH. CASH
    looks at CLAY.*

CASH. Maybe I oughta go.

CLAY. I . . . I know, Mom. I . . . uhh, Cash took a look at it.
    He's . . . giving her something.

CAROL (*to* KELLY). Did you see this?

KELLY. Um. No.

CAROL. It looks so itchy and scaly.

CLAY. It's an infection. It's a little problem.

CAROL. I wouldn't say little.

CLAY (*to* KELLY). I was just going to deal with it.

CAROL. It's all up and down the inside of her –

CLAY. Yeah, and we think. Cash and I. Or at least, *I* think it might be related to –

CAROL. Has she seen her doctor?

CLAY. Not yet.

CAROL. She needs to go to the doctor.

CLAY. I wanted to wait until I could isolate some of the potential –

CAROL. I don't think you should wait.

CLAY. *Mom! I'm not incompetent, okay?* All of you. Treating me like I'm this *failure*. Like some kind of *loser*. I know what I'm doing.

CAROL. I didn't –

CLAY. Yeah, I don't have a *job*. Is that your point? That I don't have a big desk and a big *swivel chair*, like the two of them? Well, excuse me, but who here might just have the *most important job of all*? Huh? Standing there judging me.

CAROL. We weren't judg –

CLAY. *Three hours a week*, okay? So I can go play nine holes of golf and race back here again. That's the vacation *I* get. As if any of you could know the incredible amount of *work* involved.

CAROL. I raised two children.

CLAY. And I'm trying to do a slightly less shitty job of it than you did, all right?!

Uncomfortable guilty pause. CAROL *is deeply hurt. She takes* KAYLA *off the table.* KAYLA *wanders off.*

CAROL (*to* CASH, *re. his shirt*). I'll put some Spray 'n' Wash on that.

CASH. Thanks.

> CAROL *takes the shirt and exits to the kitchen.* CASH, CLAY *and* KELLY *are left alone. Pause.*

I oughta . . . she's out there walking around in the cold.

CLAY. I mean, let's hope it's an infection, okay? Because I don't even want to contemplate what the ramifications . . . I mean, God Almighty, if someone was to hurt a child. Hurt me. Do what you want to me. But a child. An innocent . . . (*At* CASH.) *No evil in the world?* Let's hope you're right. That's all I have to say. Because otherwise . . . you know? Someone, *somewhere* is going to fucking *pay.*

> CASH *looks at* KELLY.

What?

KELLY. Oh, man.

CLAY. You think I fucked up? Is that it? I knew that's what you'd think. Go ahead. Say I fucked up. I don't care.

KELLY (*sadly*). No. It seems like you were doing the right thing.

> CLAY *is confused. He had been expecting a rebuttal.*

CLAY. Well, I was trying to.

KELLY. I'm sure you were.

CLAY. Okay.

CASH. Yeah, I don't know. Seems that way to me.

> *Pause.* KELLY *and* CASH *stare at the floor.*

CLAY. Okay, but if the two of you just stand there and . . . If I'm the only one who goes on talking, see, while the two of you just continue to stand there staring then, inevitably, right? Then how would that look? Like I'm talking because I feel . . . okay, not *guilty*, but . . . like I'm hiding something. As I talk myself into a corner. Since I . . . I mean, that's how it would *look*, right?

CASH. Not necessarily.

CLAY. And okay, maybe I'm not the perfect father, but I am *not* a sick, evil, twisted person.

KELLY (*calmly*). You're a wonderful father.

CLAY. Since I'm the only one who . . . since no one else could've . . . (*To* CASH.) I mean, you said, right? Could be any number of things. You said that. Some reaction. I don't know . . .

Phone begins to ring.

Something toxic in the . . . the Huggies, maybe. I don't know. Some kind of . . . *Jesus Christ, why the fuck am I the only person talking?!* Huh?! Why am I the only person that has anything to say?!

CAROL *has re-entered with half a loaf of bread in a plastic bag.*

CAROL. All right. Now, I admit that sometimes I get confused.

KELLY. Carol.

CAROL. But I did just hear you say you bought a *whole* loaf of this bread.

CASH. Oh Lord.

CAROL. Not a *half.*

CLAY. Oh, can we *not* go *back* to the *bread*?

CAROL. Well, I don't mean to contradict – (*To* KELLY.) – but you did say a *whole* loaf, not –

CLAY. Mom, I know you think you're helping. But when you do this? You just . . . you just . . . you just . . .

CASH. Exacerbate.

CLAY. Exacerbate the situation!

KELLY. Someone must've cut it in half, Carol.

CAROL. Well, *I* didn't. Did any of *you*?

Phone continues to ring.

Now, I know. It's just a loaf of bread.

KELLY. A *twelve-dollar* loaf of bread.

CAROL. But. If none of *us* took the missing bread. One has to assume.

CASH. Those giant rats again.

CLAY (*re. ringing phone*). Jesus, is that machine ever going to pick up?

KELLY *goes for the phone.*

CAROL. All I did was open the breadbox –

KELLY (*phone*). Hello?

CAROL. – since we don't seem to be eating dinner.

CLAY. *Why*, Mom? Why would she do that to us?

CAROL. People lash out.

CLAY. She's a quiet, shy person. She cleans the house.

KELLY (*phone*). No, no, no. Thank you. It's just a mistake.

CLAY. She looks after Kayla while I play golf. Why would she *steal* things?

CAROL. Maybe you should *ask* her why.

CLAY. *She can barely speak English!*

KELLY (*phone*). No, no. My husband broke a window, is all.

CAROL (*to* CLAY). Well, then you have to make an effort.

CLAY (*to* KELLY). Who is it?

KELLY. The alarm system automatically called the police. (*Phone.*) Yes?

KAYLA *has entered with a surprise behind her back.*

CAROL. We don't know what people are capable of.

CLAY. So we should fire her. For taking a crust of bread.

CAROL. I didn't say that at all.

KELLY (*phone*). No, he was trying to hit an animal.

CLAY. And what's more important at the moment? Protecting an innocent life? Or some idiotic . . . ?

KELLY (*phone*). No, not *our animal*. We don't *own* an animal.

CASH. *Whose* innocence are we protecting here?

CAROL (*to* KAYLA *who tugs at her sleeve*). No surprises right now, sweetheart.

CLAY (*to* KAYLA). Sweetie? Go play with Kalina, okay? Go find Kalina.

KELLY (*phone*). No. Not a pet. Arrrgh!! (*To the room.*) I swear to God, people don't even speak *English*.

CAROL. I'm only saying that if we *don't* listen to these people, these poor underprivileged people, eventually they will rise up and lash out exactly as predicted by the *Manifesto*.

CASH (*hooting with laughter*). Preach on, Comrade!

CLAY. And that is relevant *how*?

KELLY (*phone*). Excuse me. Do you have a *supervisor*?

CAROL. It could be relevant.

KELLY. Clay? Will you deal with this, please?

CAROL (*giving in to* KAYLA). Oh, all right, little miss. Let me see my surprise.

CLAY (*taking phone*). Hello? Yeah.

CAROL. Is it a special surprise? Hmm? Could it be a . . . ?

KAYLA *produces her hand from behind her back and* CAROL *jumps and runs away, waving her hands in fear.*

Oh no! No, no, no, no, no.

CLAY. What? What?

CAROL. Needle. It's a needle. No needles.

KAYLA *is holding a small hypodermic syringe with needle. The others recoil.*

KELLY (*to* CAROL). Shhh!! (*To* KAYLA.) *Kayla.* Look at Mommy. Put that down.

CLAY. Drop it, sweetie. Drop that right now.

KAYLA *shakes her head.*

KELLY (*to* CLAY). Where did she get a needle and a syringe?

CAROL. That is a nasty dirty thing.

CLAY. You drop that right this instant.

KELLY. Daddy's not kidding now.

CAROL. That is a thing that will make you sick.

KELLY. Shhh! Listen to Mommy. Listen to me.

CLAY (*phone*). Just a minute, please. (*To others.*) Whose is that? (*To* CASH.) Is that yours?

CASH. *Mine!?*

KELLY. That is not a toy. Needles are not toys.

CLAY (*to* CASH). From your *bag.* Your medical *bag.*

CASH. Who am I, *Marcus Welby?*

KELLY. Shhh!

CLAY. Well, it doesn't belong to us.

CAROL. Let's show your mommy where you found that.

KELLY. No, Carol. (*To* KAYLA.) Kayla, I mean it, now. I'm counting to three. And then *you* are going to find yourself in some *very* big trouble.

CAROL. I know she's been getting into that back room.

KELLY. One . . .

CLAY. Mom. Please. Our cleaning person is not *dispersing biological weapons.*

KELLY. Two . . .

KAYLA holds the needle up like a spear and begins chasing them, shrieking with laughter. All scream.

CAROL.	KELLY.	CLAY.	CASH.
Oh! Oh! Someone, take it from her! She's going to hurt herself or one of us! See what happens? She's lashing out! Now she's lashing out at us!	Jesus, Kayla! Stop that!! Clay, will you get that thing from her please, or do I have to do absolutely everything in this house?!	No, no, no, no! The baby! Watch out for the baby!! Kayla, you are being very, very rude and inconsiderate!	Hey hey. Don't get that thing near me. Whoa. Jesus, why don't you put a leash on this kid? Hang on. I got her.

CASH grabs KAYLA from behind. KELLY takes the needle from her, then smacks her sharply on the bottom. KAYLA glares.

KELLY. What did Mommy say to you? Mommy said no. That is a dangerous, *dangerous* thing!

CLAY. That is a *big* time out for you, little lady.

KELLY. Next time you *listen* to Mommy.

CLAY. You just got a great big time out. Right now.

KELLY. Go on. You heard what Daddy said. You go right now or we can make it *two.*

KAYLA turns and stomps up the stairs.

Pause. All stare at the needle.

CAROL (*quietly*). Well, I don't mean to jump to conclusions. But we *know* she took the bread . . .

CLAY. Why? Why hurt our *child*? Why would she?

CASH. Hey, Clay.

CAROL. We don't know. We don't know her reasons for *stealing* either.

KELLY (*handing the needle to* CLAY). I don't want to be touching this.

CAROL. But if your child is *sick*. And if she is *alone* with her.

CLAY. Look, obviously someone has done something to my child and it sure as hell wasn't *me*.

CASH. Clay?

CLAY. What?

CASH. The phone.

The lights change to isolate only CLAY *and* MR HADID. *The others exit.*

CLAY. And they put me on hold. For a minute. And you know, the mind devises these scenarios. You start to panic, and there you are on the phone with . . . the people you've *paid* to protect you. Pay your taxes to protect you. And so maybe you say something stupid without thinking. To the police. About how someone who works in your home might've done something . . . deliberately given some *sickness* . . . to a child . . . So . . . I guess . . . so, yeah, so I guess . . . well, I guess the person who said that was *me*.

MR HADID *nods*.

MR HADID (*calmly, showing no emotion throughout*). It is early evening. We are in the kitchen, myself and my wife. She has just given herself the medicine. We are about to eat. She says to me, here, look, have some of this bread. You remember this bread. We have had this before. You like this, with the figs and the nuts. I say to her, do you ask before you take this bread? Do they give you this bread, or do you

simply take it? She says, I do not ask. I take it. I say I am
sure, if you ask, they will give this to you. She says, I do
not know how to ask. I say, then I will write it down for
you. But, she says, what difference will it make for them if
I ask? I take it now. And they do not care. So I do not know
what good it does to learn.

As MR HADID *goes on talking, the others start to drift
back in. Lights change. Snow begins to fall as before.*

Then there is a knocking on the door. I stand to open it, but
before I do the policemen are inside the room. There are six
of them. They are speaking very loudly, as though I cannot
hear. I say, what is it that you want? You may come in, you
are welcome to come in, but tell me what it is that you want
to see. Then my wife begins shouting, but not English. She
says, why do you come into our home? Please leave now.
They say it is their right. And now my son runs out of his
bedroom. He has heard the noise. And he is holding the stick
of a broom. He is very angry. He says to them to get out of
our house. Leave my father and mother alone and get out.
They tell him to put down the stick. I say likewise to him,
Farah, be quiet and put down the stick. But he does not, and
so the policeman pushes my son. And suddenly everyone is
shouting. I say to them, my wife does not understand you.
She does not speak plentiful English. Tell me what to say to
her and I will say it. But still they shout, so my wife pushes
the policeman who has pushed my son.

Now we are all pushed to the floor. The handcuffs are placed
on us. We are taken down the stairs to the street. My son is
wearing only his underwear. There are three police cars
with the lights flashing. They are putting us each separate.
Each in one. I say to them, please. My wife has the diabetes.
She has taken the injection, so now she must eat. We will
co-operate with you, we are happy to do this, but please, the
medicine requires this. My son is pushed into the one car.
He says you cannot do this. You are breaking our rights. But
they roll up the window. Then my wife is in the second car.
Now I can no longer hold *my* temper. Now *I* shout at *them*.
I say, my wife must eat. Why do you not listen? And the

policeman, he takes my arm. He says, hey. Hey, buddy. *You* listen. You listen to *me*. *You* will calm down first. I say, listen, please give her something to eat. He says, listen, buddy. We will not listen until *you* are more calm. We will now go somewhere and we will listen to what you have to say after we go there. But first, buddy, *you* must be calm. You will get nothing if you do not listen to us and be calm. But I cannot be calm. If only I could. But it is hard for me, knowing that she has taken the injection and she now must eat, and so I find that I cannot be calm.

The others, minus KAYLA, have joined CLAY and MR HADID. They sip coffee. KELLY holds the BABY. A bowl of avocados now sits on the coffee table in front of them.

CAROL. And she died, then, on the way to the police station?

MR HADID. She goes into a coma. And then some time later she dies.

CAROL. It's shocking.

KELLY. Sickening.

CAROL. It's just so wrong.

KALINA. But with the police, is always the way, you know?

CAROL. Thinking that they act on our behalf. But not like *that*.

KALINA. Because of having the guns as they do, and the power.

CAROL. And when you think that at that very moment we were right here in this room.

KELLY. Without a clue what was being carried out supposedly in our names.

CAROL. And if we had just had one little conversation –

KELLY. Which of course we should have had years earlier.

CAROL. Otherwise things get misconstrued.

KELLY. Things that are over and done with.

CAROL. Silly things, really.

KELLY. Ancient history.

CAROL. But of course we don't want to hurt each other. And that's why things get left unsaid.

KALINA. But still. Was wrong, you know, this way?

KELLY (*not wanting to use the word*). Not *wrong*.

KALINA (*again, matter-of-fact*). Not to say the things. Not to say that these men, the soldiers who rape me? This is not to be ashamed. That when I was little girl and these men, they rape me, that they were to give me this sickness.

CASH. Which then . . .

KALINA (*shrugs*). Is not going to *kill* me. I just have a sickness some of the times.

CASH. Which then . . . she gives to *me* while I . . . during the period, you know, while I . . . happen to be sleeping with my brother's pregnant wife . . .

Pause.

CAROL. But when you think of *all* the terrible diseases out there.

KELLY. And which I then –

CAROL. Thank God, really, with all of the things it *could* have been.

KELLY. Which I then pass along to my daughter.

KALINA. She will have the itching some of the time, is true. Some pain and some itching.

KELLY. And that's all, thankfully.

CAROL (*raising her hand*). I had chlamydia once!

KELLY. And as long as Clay . . . as long as one's *partner* makes sure to wear a condom.

KALINA (*to* CLAY, *gently*). Yes. Always wear the condom.

CAROL. Yes.

> *All nod. Pause.* MR HADID *says nothing.* CLAY *stares at the floor.*

CASH. I mean, not to be too . . . I mean. Think about it, isn't there something almost . . . That is if the whole thing wasn't so pathetic? Really, from a certain angle . . . (*Starting to smile.*) From a *certain* perspective . . . ?

KELLY (*seeing him smile*). No. Come on. Let's not. (*To* MR HADID.) We're not. We don't . . .

CAROL. Well, yes, the truth is always a kind of *release*, isn't it?

CASH. I'm saying, c'mon. Isn't there an *element* to this that's . . . you know, just the *tiniest bit* . . . (*He chuckles.*)

CAROL. No, no, no, no, no. Now Cash? Now stop it. Now you're making me . . .

KELLY (*starting to lose it*). No, seriously. Wait, seriously?

> KELLY, CASH *and* CAROL *all giggle.*

CAROL (*to* MR HADID). Oh no, it's the discomfort. We're just *nervous.*

KELLY. Don't, because –

CAROL. Oh my goodness. It's just so *absurd.*

CASH (*laughing, to* CLAY). I mean, *how could you not know*?! Oh, come *on*! *How could you not*?!

CAROL (*to* CLAY). Remember how you were running around with the *golf club*?

KELLY (*the same*). And then you broke that window, oh my God . . .

> CLAY *looks up, unsure. A smile comes over his face. Then, slowly, he starts to join in the laughter.*

CASH. How could you not have known?! It's *preposterous.*

CAROL (*wiping away tears, to* MR HADID). We're sorry. It's just that it's so *infectious*.

The word 'infectious' cracks them all up. Only MR HADID *and* KALINA *are not laughing.*

KALINA (*staring*). I don't know. To me this is not being so funny.

The BABY *cries.* KAYLA *enters.*

KELLY (*to* KAYLA, *trying to stop laughing*). Come here, sweetie.

CAROL. Kayla! Oh, look who's here!! Come here, darling.

KELLY. Come sit with us.

CAROL. We're just being silly.

KAYLA joins them. KELLY *quietens the* BABY. *Then, they all start to notice that* CLAY, *who had been laughing, is now silently crying, with his hands covering his face. All stare.*

What is he doing? I can't tell.

KELLY. Clay.

CAROL. Is he laughing? (*To* CLAY.) Are you laughing?

KELLY. Clay, don't.

CAROL. Oh, really now.

KELLY. Please?

CAROL. I thought he was laughing.

KALINA. No. He is sad now, you see.

CAROL (*to* MR HADID). He's just being silly. (*To* KAYLA.) Your daddy's *silly*, isn't he?

KELLY. It's not the time.

CAROL. Really, it isn't.

KAYLA *tugs at* CLAY*'s sleeve. He pulls away.*

CLAY (*quietly to* KAYLA). Leave me the fuck alone.

CAROL (*admonishing*). Clay!

CLAY. I hate you all. God, I hate you all so much.

Long, long pause, while CLAY *recovers. Someone hands him a tissue. Finally,* CAROL *turns to* MR HADID.

CAROL. Anyway. We all agree, I think. That it just seems so silly to have all of these *lawyers* involved.

KELLY. And what we hoped was, that by inviting you here –

CAROL. I mean, the money is just *symbolic.*

KELLY. That we could make it about something else.

CAROL. It's a symbol. It's not what's truly important.

KELLY. What's important is the *loss*, obviously, is the *coming to terms.*

CAROL. Money isn't the same as *healing.*

KELLY. And moving on past the loss to a place of –

CAROL. – of *recovery.*

KELLY. If that makes any sense at all.

Pause.

KALINA (*confused*). Wait, is it that you now say that you are *not* to give to him the money?

KELLY (*quietly silencing* KALINA). Do you mind, please?

CAROL. No, no, no, no, no.

KELLY (*to* KALINA). We'll deal with this, okay?

CAROL (*to* MR HADID). That wasn't what we meant.

KELLY. Not in the least.

CAROL. Not at all.

KELLY. Absolutely not.

CAROL. Although . . .

KELLY. Yes. Although . . .

CAROL. When you *think* about it . . .

KELLY. I mean, my partners and I, the people from my firm, when you look at the figures *your* people quoted . . .

CAROL. We're not here to talk about figures.

KELLY. Right. However *exorbitant* those figures may be. We're talking about a *process*.

CAROL. About reaching out to one another, in this terrible terrible time, and finding a way. A simpler way . . . there's a Tibetan expression . . . ?

KELLY. We want to say we're sorry.

CAROL. Well, yes.

KALINA. But . . . I don't know why it is you don't just give to him the mon – ?

KELLY *harshly mouths the words 'Shut up' at* KALINA, *who stands and leaves the room. The rest all wait for* MR HADID *to respond.*

KELLY. So, other things aside, money aside . . .

CAROL. Now I hope we can all hear what *you* have to say.

A smile comes over MR HADID*'s face. He begins to chuckle.*

Oh, *see* . . . ?

MR HADID (*laughing*). I am sorry.

CAROL. See? That you can laugh, *too*.

KELLY. No, seriously, though.

CAROL. After all the tension and sadness. The *relief*.

KELLY. Whatever would simplify the situation. Taking the focus off the money, for the moment.

MR HADID *rises to put on his coat.*

MR HADID (*still laughing*). I am sorry.

CAROL (*realising*). Oh. Oh, wait. Oh, no.

KELLY. Why don't you just tell us how best we can salvage the, or, well, not *salvage* –

CAROL. You can't go. We have *sandwiches.*

KELLY. Maybe I should use the word *rectify.*

CASH (*to* KELLY *and* CAROL). Told you this would happen.

CAROL. Do you like grilled chicken? Or do you not eat chicken?

KELLY. Or let's use *your* terms, then. Whatever your terms are.

CASH (*to* MR HADID). But you know what, *Hajji*? In some countries? When you come into a person's *home*?

CAROL. Or we could make you one with something else.

MR HADID *raises his hand.*

MR HADID (*with finality*). I am sorry.

He heads for the door.

CAROL. Oh no. This is awful. Oh no.

KELLY (*rising and following him*). Let's say this. Let's say you and I review the figures. Because maybe there's something I'm missing. Maybe I'm not seeing it in the correct light.

CASH (*calling after him*). There is a thing known as *courtesy,* my friend!

MR HADID *is gone.* KELLY *calls back to* CLAY *as she follows him out.*

KELLY. Thank you, Clay. Thank you for your contribution.

Now KELLY *is gone, leaving the front door open.*

CAROL. Oh, how disappointing. After all that.

CASH. Smug little bastard.

CAROL. To have it end like that.

CASH. Sanctimonious little prick.

CAROL. After going to all this trouble. Ohh. That's very unsatisfying.

Pause. KAYLA *kicks her feet a bit.*

CASH (*to* CAROL). Grilled chicken and what else?

CAROL. Pesto, I think?

CASH. I like pesto.

CAROL. Mm-hmm.

CASH. Is there cheese?

CAROL. Clay made them. You'll have to look.

CASH *rises and exits.*

(*Shaking her head.*) Mm-mm-mm. Sometimes I wonder why we even *try.*

We hear a car start up and drive away. Pause. CAROL *looks at her watch.*

(*To* CLAY.) What's your PBS station here? Is it Channel Eleven?

CLAY *nods.* CAROL *moves to the TV.* KELLY *returns to the door, talking on her cellphone.*

KELLY (*phone*). No, we tried. Total waste of time. No, he didn't go for it.

CAROL *is trying to use the remote.* KAYLA *reaches into the bowl on the table and picks up an avocado. She sits again, to* CLAY's *side.*

No, we said all the right things. At least, *I* thought we did.

CAROL *turns on the TV but somehow, instead of PBS, she has managed to turn on the porn.*

CAROL. Oh, no. No, no, no. Wait. Oh, poop, here we go again. *Clay?*

KELLY (*phone*). No, I think we're screwed.

CAROL (*re. TV*). Does anybody know how to stop this?

KAYLA *tugs at* CLAY's *sleeve. He turns to look at her. Holding the avocado like an apple, she bites deeply into it and holds it up for* CLAY *to see. Lights and TV fade to black.*

End of play.

Mark O'Rowe
FROM BOTH HIPS & THE ASPIDISTRA CODE
HOWIE THE ROOKIE
MADE IN CHINA
TERMINUS

Suzan-Lori Parks
TOPDOG/UNDERDOG

Drew Pautz
SOMEONE ELSE'S SHOES

Tanya Ronder
BLOOD WEDDING *after* Lorca
MACBETT *after* Ionesco
PERIBANEZ *after* Lope de Vega
VERNON GOD LITTLE *after* DBC Pierre

Jack Thorne
STACY & FANNY AND FAGGOT
WHEN YOU CURE ME

Enda Walsh
BEDBOUND & MISTERMAN
DISCO PIGS & SUCKING DUBLIN
THE SMALL THINGS
THE WALWORTH FARCE

Nicholas Wright
CRESSIDA
HIS DARK MATERIALS *after* Pullman
MRS KLEIN
THE REPORTER
THERESE RAQUIN *after* Zola
VINCENT IN BRIXTON
WRIGHT: FIVE PLAYS

A Nick Hern Book

The Pain and the Itch first published in Great Britain
as a paperback original in 2007 by Nick Hern Books Limited,
14 Larden Road, London W3 7ST in association with
the Royal Court Theatre, London

The Pain and the Itch copyright © 2007 Bruce Norris

Bruce Norris has asserted his right to be identified as
the author of this work

Cover illustration by Nate Williams; designed by Feast Creative
Cover designed by Ned Hoste, 2H

Typeset by Country Setting, Kingsdown, Kent CT14 8ES
Printed in the UK by CPI Bookmarque, Croydon, CR0 4TD

A CIP catalogue record for this book is available from
the British Library

ISBN 978 1 85459 584 3